A Man Among Them: The Les Ollila Story

By Judi Coats

Foreword by Dr. James D. Bennett
Life and Testimony of Dr. Paul Patz, Founder of Northland Baptist Bible College

A Man Among Them:
The Les Ollila Story

Foreword by Dr. James D. Bennett

ISBN 0-9748259-0-5

Includes bibliographical references

Printed in the United States of America

Dedication

This work is dedicated to my family; they patiently and prayerfully waited and watched in the wings for the completion of this biography. My husband Dave and our three children—Julie, Jennie, and Jon—have been my constant encouragers. My mother, Hilda Sand, has been my faithful proofreader and cheerleader.

And finally, the book is dedicated to Pastor Timothy Collard for his inspiration to pour myself into this worthy project.

SPECIAL ACKNOWLEDGEMENTS

Special thanks to Michigan's Houghton County Historical Society for the permission to use the cover photo of a copper mine village (called a *location*)—The photo is from the late eighteen hundreds.

Special thanks to Adam Blumer, Luke Bolton, Elizabeth Curtis, and the publication crew of Northland Baptist Bible College for helping me to organize and to categorize all of the photographs—Adam, you are a tremendous blessing to me.

Special thanks to my fellow English teachers at Northland who encouraged me through these two and a half years of research—thanks for your friendship.

Special thanks to Les and Charlene who opened their home numerous times for me to come over to "bug" them with questions—and special thanks to the rest of their family and friends for patience with my interviewing all of them—You made me feel welcome.

Special thanks to Dr. William Knox and Dr. Ray Ventre, my teachers and mentors, who did nothing but encourage me throughout my research project.

FOREWORD

By Dr. James D. Bennett

Life and Testimony of Dr. Paul Patz,
Founder of Northland Baptist Bible College

Papa Patz

Foreword
Introduction

St. Paul's in London is one of the world's great cathedrals and the masterpiece of the famous architect, Sir Christopher Wren. Besides the massive dome and famous whispering gallery, numerous tombs and memorials beautifully adorn the magnificent structure. Almost out of character with its opulent surroundings is the simple marble slab marking the final resting place of Sir Christopher Wren. Above the slab is a simple inscription "lector, si monumentum requiris, circumspice" (reader, if you seek his monument, look around you).

Surrounded by national forest land in an isolated spot in northeast Wisconsin, one might not immediately grasp the affinity and relevance of this inspiring London monument. But then, fully grasping the life and legacy of Paul Patz is not a simple proposition either. It has been said that an institution is often merely the lengthened shadow of a man. This saying is certainly true of Northland Baptist Bible College in Dunbar, Wisconsin. One could echo Sir Christopher Wren's inscription: "If you seek Paul Patz's monument, look around you."

In the summer of 1983, the board of Northland Mission, Inc. was searching for a president for Northland Baptist Bible College to replace the former president, Dr. James Wooster, who had been called to the mission field of Haiti. As a result, Les Ollila found himself sitting across from the members of the board, laboring through the necessary interview process. As the meeting progressed, he posed a simple question: "Why is Northland here?" By Les's own testimony, the answer he got from Dr. Paul Patz was more than enough to convince him that the hand of God was on this ministry to which he was now being called. What were these powerful words that would prove so crucial in his decision? The next few pages retell that powerful message, the life and testimony of Paul Patz.

The Life of Paul Patz, Northland Baptist Bible College's Founder

The story of John and Augusta Patz and their ten children is the story of typical immigrant families that came to America at the turn of the twentieth century in search of a better life. John and Augusta were married in their native Russia in 1890 but later moved to Romania to find work. After hearing of the abundant opportunities in America, John decided that he should go to America while Augusta and their four children should return to Russia awaiting the call from John once he was established. John Patz arrived in the vicinity of Beaver, Wisconsin, in 1900 at the age of 31. It was not until July 4, 1902, that the other five members of his family joined him. Over the next eleven years, six more children were added to the Patz family. On April 27, 1911, the ninth child, Paul, was born. Born into a home of poverty and hardship, Paul would display a commitment and loyalty to this home that God would later bless in a most unusual way.

There was much to test the loyalty of Paul Patz in his youth. John would often return to the family farm in a drunken stupor. As his father stumbled through the door, Paul would rise and tend to the horses regardless of the time of night. This pattern of drunkenness only increased the pressures felt by the struggling family. It fell upon Augusta to lead the family in spiritual matters. Paul fondly recalled the hours his mother would spend reading the Bible to her children. It was like having their own Sunday school at home. Augusta's pattern of Bible reading and prayer would continue to benefit a third generation of Patz children as Augusta spent her final years in the home of Paul until she finally died in 1975 at the age of 104!

Death did come prematurely to some members of the family. Five-year-old Gust died of diphtheria in 1904. The death that took the greatest toll on Paul was the passing of Elmer, his older brother of four years. The year was 1922 and Paul was eleven at the time. He somberly recalled that the bed once shared by three brothers was now shared by only two. The consequences of Elmer's death went beyond the normal pangs felt over the loss of a loved one. Now, at the age of eleven, Paul became the primary laborer on a one-hundred-sixty-acre farm. Paul learned the value of hard work early in life.

The demands of farm life had never allowed Paul to pursue much education. His earliest memory of farm life is of watching other children go to school while he was forced to toil the day in farm work, clearing land and digging potatoes. The first opportunity for any formal education came to Paul when he was seven. The town of Beaver had a one-room schoolhouse known as the White Potato Lake School. Though they were primitive by modern standards (there was no indoor plumbing), these accommodations were an enjoyable distraction from farm chores. However, Paul was never able to complete a single year from start to finish. The demands of the harvest never allowed him to begin school before October. In addition, fields without fences meant the spring thaw would force him to leave school to watch the cows. This pattern continued for three years.

In the classroom, Paul faced other obstacles besides his sporadic attendance. At home, his parents spoke Polish, Russian, and German. The Patz children primarily spoke a Polish/Russian dialect but did manage to learn the rudiments of German because, as Paul remembered, his parents would speak German with visiting friends about things they wished to keep hidden from the kids. Since most children throughout the community spoke Polish, Russian, German, or Swedish, the first year of schooling was designed to introduce the children to the English language. The linguistic barrier compounded by the strenuous work on the farm made the months he did spend in school very difficult. All attempts to overcome these obstacles were set aside in 1922 when Elmer died. With Elmer's death, Paul's formal education ended. He had not made it past the third grade. This lack of formal education created in Paul a sense of inadequacy that never left him.

Church had always been a luxury in this farming community. The younger children would frequently attend a Sunday afternoon Bible class conducted by the oldest sister, Alma. These classes were held outdoors or in neighborhood homes, and all the children of the community were invited. Traveling the seven miles to the church in the village of Pound could be extremely difficult, especially in the winter. Nevertheless, Augusta faithfully encouraged her children to attend the services at the church and required them to attend the countryside cottage meetings when they were held.

Cottage meetings were not unique to the area. Many rural communities across America benefited from the services of an itinerant preacher from a nearby village. In 1928 Henry Schilke was the pastor of First Baptist Church in Pound, Wisconsin, a position he held for twenty-seven years. It was at a cottage meeting led by Reverend Schilke and held at the Patz farm that the conviction of the Holy Spirit became evident in the life of Paul. A conversation after the meeting between Pastor Schilke and Paul failed to produce an immediate response. However, the evening chores took Paul out in the field to bring the cows home for the night. While out in the field, he knelt and wept behind a big pine stump with the conviction of knowing he was "a Hell-bound sinner." Still, however, his soul found no peace. He engaged in continuous prayer all day Monday, Tuesday, and Wednesday to no avail.

That Wednesday night a meeting called the faithful to church, and on this evening the church was voting on candidates for baptism. Part of the examination involved answering a series of questions. When Reverend Schilke asked Paul if he had asked God to forgive him of his sins, he answered yes; and the congregation greeted the news of his "salvation" with joy. Nevertheless, Paul left the meeting with the same frustration and uncertainty with which he had arrived.

The following day Paul was once again out in the fields plowing with his father. When his father left for a time, Paul was given the opportunity to go to the Lord once again with his frustrations. Paul remembered "praying as I had never prayed before." In that field, on a warm August day in 1928, Paul Patz was saved by the grace of God. The proofs of his salvation were immediately evident to Paul. Not only did he have the promise of God's word, but he also had an unusual peace in his soul. Something else his salvation brought was an intense burden to serve the Lord. As he later explained, "I lost one burden and picked up another load." This "load" perplexed Paul. After all, what could God ever do with someone with only a third-grade education?

Any student of American history knows that 1929 was the beginning of a very difficult period for the American people. Survival could no longer be taken for granted in the land of plenty. News stories emerged of families surviving on spoiled vegetables or wild dandelions. One report in 1933 totaled as many as 29 people dead from simple starvation in New York City alone. Among the hardest hit were the midwestern farmers. Across America, the farmer's struggle to stay solvent would often turn violent as desperate men brandished pitchforks and shotguns in an effort to close down courts and disrupt mortgage auctions. In the midst of these dark days, God was doing something very special on a small depression-laden farm in northeast Wisconsin.

The situation on the Patz farm had not seemed so bleak a few years earlier. In 1919, Paul's oldest brother Charlie had returned from France where he had served during the Great War. With his help, work was begun on a new 4,000 square-foot barn. The labor of building a barn and collecting the stones for an accompanying two-foot wall seemed bearable with the combined effort of John and his four boys. The future of the Patz family farm seemed bright.

However, Elmer was taken just three years later in 1922. Charlie left the farm at age 27 to get married and to work in an automobile plant in Detroit. Harry left the farm at the age of fifteen, also convinced that life in the city would bring greater returns. He, too, went to Detroit, where he was employed by a Ford plant (both Harry and Charlie would return to the area during the Depression after losing their jobs). Shortly after Harry left, John left for Washington to be with his brother Mike. He was gone for two and a half years. When he finally returned, he bore the scars of a stroke. In his debilitated condition, he would never again work the fields or tend the livestock. Thus, at the age of eighteen, Paul was the only laborer on a struggling farm laden with the additional burden of a heavy mortgage.

Numerous friends urged Paul to abandon the farm and look for work elsewhere. This seemed to be the sensible thing to do. As he contemplated his future, Paul was approached by his mother who pleaded with him to stay and work the family farm. "If you will stay and honor my wishes" she told him, "someday you will have more than all the others [his brothers and sisters] combined." Ignoring all other advice, Paul chose to honor the wishes of his mother and stay on the family farm. It turned out that Augusta was right. God honors faithfulness.

During the coming depression, Paul almost lost the family farm on a number of occasions. The defining moment came in 1933. In the midst of a seven-year drought and with the depression peaking, the owner of the farm's mortgage told Paul that he must assume responsibility for the full finances of the farm. Ignoring the economic realities of the situation and still desiring to honor the wishes of his parents, Paul received the deed to the farm and the heavy mortgage, which he liked to remember, was "eleven years older than myself." The weight and pressures of this farm were fast becoming more than one man could bear. Yet his natural optimism and inclination to work hard were about to be rewarded, for he would soon have help on the farm.

Paul had known Mamie Stank since she was a youth. However, their age difference (he was five years older than Mamie) had made her simply one of the many farm girls who lived over the hills from the family farm. Things began to change in 1933 as Paul's visits to the Stank farm became more frequent. Finally, on November 20, 1935, he married the twin daughter of Mr. and Mrs. Gust Stank at the Section Eight Baptist Church in Pound, Wisconsin. The happy marriage would produce seven children and last almost fifty-nine years. For the first few years of marriage, the two would live on the family farm with his parents. By 1941, they were able to build a house of their own on the existing farm property. The original cost of the home was $3,700. The work contribution of Mamie was immediately apparent. Paul and Mamie not only improved the farm in the coming years but also amazingly had paid off the entire mortgage by 1945! They lived for many years in their first home. It was not until 1962 that a new home would be built. By this time, the couple had seven children.

The absence of debt did not mean the absence of rigorous labor. One of the incessant tasks Paul faced each day was shoveling and hauling manure. Throughout the late 1930s and early 1940s, he had experimented in a local blacksmith shop owned by Clarence Graetz with an idea for improving the Lauden manure carrier he used on the farm. At the time, this carrier was the standard in the industry. Its design was simple. It was a large bucket operated by a hoist hung from a track on the ceiling of the barn. The manure was loaded into the bucket and then pushed by hand out of the barn into a waiting pit. Paul improved this carrier in 1940 by inventing a motorized attachment with a reversible switch. He applied for and received a patent in 1942. He then attempted to sell this patent to the Lauden company. For three years he was denied a response. He later learned the company was working on a similar attachment. The experience was a great lesson for Paul. He promised God if He ever allowed him to invent anything else, he would go into business for himself. Indeed, the hand of God was soon to become very evident in this endeavor.

From 1946 to 1947, Paul began work on a new barn cleaner that used a gutter rather than a bucket. He again went to Greatz blacksmith shop where he sketched three different models. His hard work produced three experimental cleaners that he installed on his farm and two others. In 1946, a neighbor along with an engineer from a manufacturing company came to Paul's barn in his absence and copied the shuttle stroke design of the barn cleaner without his permission. A second time, *man* was attempting to cheat Paul out of success. However, the schemes of man are powerless to arrest the designs of God. Unbeknownst to the two men, the design that would revolutionize the industry sat safely in the barn of Paul's neighbor, Gust Tachick.

By 1947, there were five new manufacturers of gutter barn cleaners, but each faced a series of common problems. They all needed two motors, two chains, and a deep pit into which the manure could drop. One unit would clean the gutters and make the complete sweep through the barn. But because of the design of the chain, a second unit was necessary for elevating the manure to allow it to be carried out of the barn and automatically loaded onto manure spreaders. It was the special hook and eye chain link invented by Paul Patz that solved these problems. The link was able to flex in all directions allowing Paul to invent a barn cleaner with one motor, one reducer, and one chain. This chain made it possible to elevate the slide of the cleaner to a degree that made a pit unnecessary. Believing the cleaner would sell, he went into business in 1948.

The business started small. The cleaners were produced in the blacksmith shop of Clarence Graetz that was now converted into a machine shop. Paul himself was the first Patz Company salesman making his first sale in Gillet, Wisconsin, to Joe Kershek. In the coming days, a handful of cleaners would be sold to other neighbors; and by the end of 1949, his second year in business, Paul had sold over 200 cleaners. The future once again seemed promising.

The Patz family needed good news in those days. One year earlier, Paul's father John had died of heart failure. A few months later, two-year-old Eleanor, the youngest daughter of Paul and Mamie, had contracted polio. Her life was spared, but she would bear the scars of the polio for the rest of her life. The lessons learned by Paul and Mamie at this time would be valuable as this was to be the beginning of a series of physical struggles the family would be forced to endure. Mamie would suffer from diabetes after the birth of Darrell in 1955 until her death in 1994. The member of the family who would suffer most, however, was Paul himself.

In March of 1947, Paul went to a dentist in Peshtigo, to have two teeth extracted and several teeth filled. When his tongue was accidentally pricked, a painful lesion began to form. The constant pain and fever led him to consult many doctors throughout 1948 and 1949. Finally, in February 1950, he visited Dr. Jones, a throat specialist in Menominee, Michigan. The doctor cut a tissue sample from the lesion and sent it off for analysis. One week later the results were in. Paul had cancer of the tongue. Not surprisingly, he attacked the cancer with the same determination he had attacked every challenge with which he had been confronted in his life.

An initial surgery was performed at Marinette General Hospital. The excision of the cancer involved the cutting and stitching of the tongue. As the owner of a new business, Paul could not take the normal period for recuperation. Less than one week after the surgery, he was out servicing barn installations. Even after his tongue healed, it was weak and painful. This condition made it very difficult for Paul to speak and led to greater feelings of inadequacy.

In 1951, the cancer reoccurred. A trip to Mayo Clinic in Rochester, Minnesota, resulted in a second cancer surgery. After the surgery, Paul was sent to a hospital in Green Bay for follow-up x-rays. Performed in October 1951, the x-rays burned both his neck and face so that he was not presentable for several weeks. Continued problems with his tongue led him to Windsor, Ontario, to seek treatment. The treatment involved frequent injections into the bloodstream. These injections necessitated traveling from Pound to Windsor four different times during the winter and spring months. The treatments seemed to keep the cancer in remission until 1955 when it appeared again. In July, Paul had another surgery to remove the cancer. Realizing the surgeries were not stopping the cancer, he next consulted the Hoxsey Cancer Clinic in Dallas, Texas. During the next thirty months, he made five trips to Dallas for examination.

From 1950 to 1982, Paul would have 25 cancer surgeries in various clinics and hospitals. In the course of these surgeries, he lost many of his teeth, parts of his jawbone, and half of his tongue. Communication became extremely difficult. Simple activities such as eating and drinking became difficult. By his own confession, Paul would admit that this condition left him in a "predicament not possible to explain." In all these trials, he could feel the Lord strengthening his faith in Him. He was sustained by the understanding that he was "safe in the arms of the Great Physician."

The demands of the business had not ceased during these difficult times. By 1951, Paul realized that he needed his own plant. He purchased two acres and constructed a 60' by 112' building. As the business grew, so did the facility. In 1953 and again in 1958, a 120' by 112' addition was added. Then in 1963, a 202' by 202' expansion was completed. Today, the Patz Company has a little over five acres under a single roof. At its peak employment in 1979, it employed 440 workers, making it the largest business of its kind in the industry and one of the largest employers of any type in Marinette County, Wisconsin.

One key to success was Paul's determination to keep his inventive mind active. The barn cleaner was the first of many inventions. In 1953, he invented a silage unloader. Material movers, cattle feeders, manure spreaders, manure stackers, silage carts, and blower pipe clamps were to follow.

With only a third-grade education, Paul Patz became a pioneer in the farm equipment industry.

In the 1980s, the sag in the agricultural industry compelled the Patz Company to begin manufacturing non-agricultural goods. In the last few years, they filled contracts for numerous businesses, and by 1999 as much as 15% of the business was non-agricultural in nature. Today, Patz equipment and manufactured goods can be found all across the country and in numerous foreign countries including Canada, Japan, Switzerland, Denmark, Australia, and New Zealand.

Even as God prospered the Patz Company, He had another major test for Paul and his family. Though the devastation could have been much worse if not for the quick action of a number of employees, an entire wing of the Patz factory burned on February 11, 1971. Fire departments from seven different communities spent over three hours bringing the blaze under control. Damages originally estimated at $600,000 eventually spiraled to $1,000,000. By God's strength, Paul Patz viewed each obstacle as a chance to see God work in an unusual way. In the wake of the fire, his testimony remained as solid as it had ever been. He was quoted in the local paper as stating, "I have placed faith in God in the past and will continue to do so. I am confident He will take care of us."

As Paul traveled throughout northeast Wisconsin and the upper peninsula of Michigan, he began to develop a burden for the unreached communities of the region.

Since his conversion, he had felt a burden to be involved in ministry but felt inadequate to participate directly. However, as God prospered his business, it became evident to him that one way he could contribute to a variety of ministries was through financial support.

It was at a meeting of the Northern Baptist Convention that Paul sat under the ministry of someone he remembered only as Mr. Kraft. Like Paul, he owned his own business; and as he challenged those in the audience to give out of their abundance, Paul became more determined than ever to use the profits of Patz Sales Incorporated for the work of the ministry. He had always been a loyal contributor to the ministries of his local church. Now in his excitement, he became the catalyst for paying off the mortgage of the First Baptist Church. His giving to missionaries and other established ministries was also increased. And then, in 1958, he began to contemplate using his resources to develop a new ministry. After much prayer and consultation with his family, Paul decided to build a camp for young people. It was Mamie's idea to call the new venture "Northland," for it seemed to her an accurate description.

Paul approached an attorney who had been used by the Patz Company on a number of occasions. When told by Paul of his intent to launch this new venture, the attorney promised to complete the necessary paperwork for the Patz family. Paul anxiously waited for months to receive the papers. By December 28, the papers had not been received; and the window to make a contribution to the new ministry was closing. When he called the Madison office of the attorney, Paul was informed that the attorney was on vacation until January 10th. Paul believed that the attorney never had any intention of filing those papers.

With this apparent setback, Paul became discouraged. God had prospered the business that year in an unusual way, and the time was right to make an immediate contribution. He decided to seek help from an old lawyer friend to see if anything could be done. This friend put Paul in contact with an attorney from Green Bay who promised to help in any way he could. Amazingly, twenty-four hours later, the legal papers were complete; and Paul personally drove to Madison to file them with the state offices. Having done this, Northland Mission Incorporated was now officially organized on December 30, 1958, and recorded in the office of the Register of Deeds in Marinette, Wisconsin. Its stated purpose was to establish and operate a summer camp with the intention that its facilities would be used for other religious, educational, and charitable purposes.

Northland Mission Camp

Throughout much of 1959, Paul searched many places for suitable land for the construction of the campsite. He first selected a site near his home in Pound; but when the potential sellers discovered his intended use for the property, they refused to sell. His search took him next to a piece of property located in the town of Dunbar, approximately 40 miles north of Pound. The land had belonged to a Patz dealer from Madison. The man was involved in a car accident and had died from his injuries. Paul approached the father of the widow (who was now handling her financial affairs) and made him an offer. The man demanded $2000, and Paul responded that he would be willing to put the money in escrow awaiting the transfer of the deed to the land.

Satan was now attempting to hinder Paul a second time through a series of discouraging setbacks. It was discovered that the deceased man had married his current wife without her knowledge of a previous wife. It was the name of the first wife that appeared on the deed, and she now flatly refused to sign off. Despite making a down payment on the land in October of 1959, eleven months would pass; and Paul would still not have a cleared deed to the land. He began to contemplate rescinding his offer. Once again, he was forced to give his anxiety to the Lord and let Him show Himself mighty. This he did, and just one month later the deed to the property was in Paul's hands. He was not sure how the other parties worked out their differences.

The incident had delayed construction by a year; but in the fall of 1960, work began on the main buildings. The construction blueprints were simple adaptations of the pencil sketches Paul had given to Krause lumber in

Coleman when he first began mentally developing the property. By the summer of 1961, a 400-seat dining hall and one dorm were completed; and camp was officially begun. The work was completed under the direction of Ed Beiber, a man with whom Paul had nothing more than a "gentleman's agreement" as to the work expectations.

Throughout the 1960s, various churches and groups used the campground for their camping program. In 1967, Northland Mission started a summer camping program consisting of one week known as "Key to Life." It was this program that provided the foundation for Northland Camp and Conference Center. Since the camping facility opened its doors almost 40 years ago, thousands of lives have been changed because of the vision and sacrifice of Paul Patz. To date, over 75,000 campers have passed through the Northland camping facility!

It was during the early 1970s, that the Patz family began considering ways in which the camping facilities could be used in a fuller, year-round capacity. The second phase of the development of the ministry—a Bible college—was the result of Paul's desire to give lower-class kids of northeast Wisconsin something he never had: a formal education. The culmination of that burden is an institution of higher learning in the north woods of Wisconsin now known as Northland Baptist Bible College. Since it opened in 1976, thousands of students have come to this college to be better equipped to spread the good news of the gospel that changed the life of Paul Patz at the age of 17. It is a message of hope. It is a message that delivers men from the bondage of sin. It is the wonderful story that God so loved the world that he gave His only begotten Son that whosoever believeth on Him should not perish, but have everlasting life.

The life of Paul Patz reminds us of many things. It reminds us that God is a rewarder of those that diligently seek him. It reminds us that true success is not measured in dollars and cents. It reminds us that God is no respecter of persons and that He will use anyone to further His cause on this earth. In his final days, the memory that seemed most vivid to Paul was an event from the summer of 1961. He was attending a preaching service at the newly opened campground in Dunbar. It was there, he remembers, that it hit him; "I am in the ministry!" Yes, Paul Patz was in the ministry. Literally, the sun never sets on the graduates that have been sent from Northland Baptist Bible College and the campers that have attended Northland Camp and Conference Center. His ministry was one of vision and provision that continues to make it possible for so many to hear of the love of God that is freely offered to a world of sinful men. "Reader, if you seek his monument, look around you."

Augusta Patz, Paul's Mother

The early days of the Patz Company

A rapidly growing Patz Company

1971 Patz Company fire

Firefighters battle 1971 blaze

Blaze destroys large part of Patz Company

Paul Patz watches 1971 blaze

Paul observes fire's destruction

Patz Company plant

Patz Company product

The plant in Coleman

Papa Patz and his sons

Papa, Mamie, and children

Paul and Mamie Patz

50th anniversary family celebration

1981 Founder's Day

Papa's personal touch

A thankful Papa observing
God's blessings on Northland

Breaking ground for the Jacquot Educational Center

Dr. Paul Patz

Paul and Sadie Patz

AUTHOR'S NOTE

The following pages are filled with the anecdotal record of Dr. Leslie Ollila's life. The goal in writing the chapters in frame-story format came as a result of the desire to have the biography sound like the storyteller that Dr. Ollila exemplifies. Most of the book is pieced together from the numerous interviews that I conducted over two years along with research of the area in which Dr. Ollila grew up. All story content is a compilation of information from the many interviews in addition to an interview with Les Ollila himself. Otherwise, specific quotations are used from interviews to shed light on a story from various individuals' personal experience. This research project set forth to investigate not only the county where the subject grew up, but it also set forth to gather information from the various relatives and friends of the man, Leslie Ollila. Several months of investigation were needed to study the area of Calumet, Michigan, of the Upper Peninsula, which is Dr. Ollila's birthplace. Because Dr. Ollila is Finnish, I needed to study the Finnish ways as they manifested themselves as a part of the environment of specifically, Gratiot Location, the hometown of Dr. Ollila. Also, my interviews were conducted via email, via phone, via letter, and in person as well. After transcribing almost ninety interviews and reading Internet sources and books with information containing the historical backgrounds of the Copper Country, the

Charlene was given morphine for the pain, and the medical team concluded that she was not having a heart attack; so they would do further testing. A CAT Scan was scheduled next. Steven and Lisa drove home to gather a few things for their mother and to prepare to return some time later in the day. Tami told Charlene that she was going to make a quick visit to Wal-mart across the street, and she would promptly return to Charlene's room where the hospital intended to admit and treat her mother. Little Haley, Tami's youngest, accompanied her mother because Tami was still nursing her and it was difficult to leave her with anyone. So Charlene was off for more testing, Tami to do some shopping, and Lisa and Steven were on the road home.

Meanwhile, on the Los Angeles freeway, Les and John David Ollila, Marty Von, and Sam Horn were facing the traffic on their way to the airport. This was a typical scenario for them as they traveled extensively speaking and counseling. Les loved to take his grandson, John David (or JD as they call him), who was fifteen years old, along to spend time with him to show JD diversity of culture and to have him meet numbers of Les's friends. At the moment, the multi-laned traffic rushing to Los Angeles kept them focused on getting to their destination.

Tami parked on the east side of the hospital and made her way through the automatic doors with Haley on one hip, her mom's and her purses over one shoulder, and a blue plastic Wal-mart bag hanging from her other wrist.

Tami had been gone a little longer than she had wanted to but needed to get a list of things for herself and her mom. She had remembered the number of the room where the emergency receptionist had said her mom would be, so she rode the elevator to that floor. Juggling her armful was the least of her concerns at that moment. She paced her steps past the restroom door down to the specific wing and past the nurses' station. She quietly slipped into the room where her mom was supposed to be resting, but Tami found the room empty.

Returning at once to the nurses' station, Tami waited as the three nurses discussed another patient and his needs. When they looked up, Tami inquired about the lady that was supposed to be in the empty room. The nurses' heads jerked up at each other and their eyes told Tami that her mother's status had changed somehow for the worse. The room swirled around Tami's ears for a split second and she had to keep her balance with her load in each arm and not forget that she was holding her own daughter. Her mind told her that her mother was either dead or at the point of dying. A nurse, someone Tami had seen and known before stepped out from behind the desk, and she told Tami that she would take her downstairs. She lightened Tami's load by holding Haley and the packages. In the stairwell, a private place that the nurse chose to take Tami downstairs, she stopped her and put her arm on Tami and gently broke the news to her: "Your mom is about to die. You need to go down and say

This decision turned out to be a life-changing decision. If Charlene had flown by emergency air ambulance that day, her aorta would have burst completely because of the air pressure, and she never would have survived for certain. Before the ambulance departed, Lisa and Tami had to say their last good-byes because the doctors genuinely felt that their mother would not survive the trip down to Green Bay. The Ollila daughters carefully chose their last loving words to their mother.

Steven, however, didn't make it back to Iron Mountain to the hospital. He jumped into his car to make the journey to Green Bay to meet up with his mother there. On the way, Charlene's ambulance sped by him in Wausaukee. On that 100-mile trip from Iron Mountain to Green Bay, the ambulance sped under stormy skies and over wet roads. Steven tried to keep pace behind in his car with his thoughts swirling. Riding down in a separate car with her husband, Brian, Lisa struggled with her emotions. Tami said that she cried out loud to God:

> *Okay, God, here we are. Help me if I get to the hospital and my mom is dead. Help me to know that you are in control and that you are sovereign and that your way is perfect; I know it in my head, but I want to know it in my heart. And I kept praying that over and over because that would have been the hardest situation that I would have had to face because my mom and I are so close.*

When Lisa got in touch with her dad, he was on a cell phone driving down the Los Angeles freeway. This call was made prior to the diagnosis of the split aorta. Lisa relates, "What happened was that I had to call dad from Iron Mountain and I got ahold of him and I said, 'Mom is in the hospital—nothing major—they are running tests. It isn't her heart,' and I said, 'They are going to admit her and I wanted you to know.'" That early contact with her dad came before his daughter really knew what was going on. Within hours, Les, JD, Marty, and Sam boarded the plane to Minneapolis where they would change planes to come home to Green Bay.

In California, Les had gone to direct a leadership conference with Pastor Chapel and his staff. The trip was actually two-fold because the administrative team members from Northland Baptist Bible College were also meeting with Pastor Matt Olson in Denver who would succeed Les as president of Northland Baptist Bible College. Charlene and Susan Von who had accompanied their husbands had just returned to Dunbar from that trip to Denver to meet Matt Olson while Les and Marty had gone on to California with Sam Horn and John David. Marty Von related:

> *Dr. O has always been anxious to help young pastors who have a heart for the Lord and have a heart for soul winning and a heart for evangelism, so he conferred with me on whether or not we should do this meeting with Dr. Chapel. He felt*

This was a shocking report for Marty to receive. He found Sam and told him the news, and they decided that Sam would take John David for a walk while Marty talked to Les.

Marty's mind raced as this was undoubtedly the most difficult news that he would have to break to his lifelong friend. Marty had lived through a death in his own family. He recalled having to tell his own father that his grandfather had passed away. Those memories rushed through his mind. He knew that Les could read him and so, as he paced those steps to the departure gate, he asked God for wisdom that when he would speak God would fill his mouth. He cried out, "How am I going to relate this news to my friend?" Marty caught up with Les at the gate where the plane for Green Bay was to depart in just seven minutes. Marty's eyes could not hold back tears and Les knew immediately that his friend was deeply struggling. "Les, I'm really afraid. I'm really afraid. I'm afraid for Charlene. They've had to take her to Green Bay and it looks like an aneurism of the heart." He wanted to make the news serious but also give him some hope.

Sam Horn explained to the ticket agent the dilemma and the airlines held the departure—an unprecedented situation. Marty suggested that Les call Lisa. Lisa said that she was able to keep her composure and explain to her dad that the ambulance had taken Mom to Green Bay and the doctors would take her into surgery to try to repair damage to the heart. Marty said that the very first words out of Les's mouth upon hearing the news were these: "God is sovereign—He is in control."

Once on the plane, Les sat at a window seat, Marty sat on the aisle, and JD and Sam sat across the aisle. They still had not broken all the news to John David. Marty relates from those moments:

> *Our heads were bowed. We prayed together and in my years of traveling with Dr. O, there are times that he is being touched by God and needs time to think or interpret what God is speaking to him about. My only words to him in that fifty-minute flight were "I'm praying for you." He did not respond because his head was down and turned toward the window. Les spent the entire trip in a frozen position with his head bowed and looking out the window. My sense was that he was totally consumed with praying and asking God for his help and grace. Dr. Horn and I confirmed that our prayer was that God would spare Charlene's life. At this desperate state, we begged God to spare her life.*

The reflection in the plane window was a rugged, dedicated man's face with tears filling the lines of late middle-age and eyes that sought the face of God to keep his companion of thirty-nine years alive—the one whom he loved dearly.

10). The beautiful Lake Superior borders all of these towns. Mohawk became a village in the early 1900's and the mining companies owned homes in *locations* as they called them, and they sold the houses to employees but kept the land in the company's possession. The Einard Ollilas rented a home in Gratiot Location in the early 1900's and leased it for 99 years. Technically, the house is still theirs today.

These were the days of axes felling trees, miners digging in the earth for rich copper, and contractors building elaborate homes along the main street of Calumet to house wealthy mining company owners. The bustling Calumet streets were laden with miners carrying lunch pails rushing between shifts. "Only sixteen years before [the discovery of copper] Calumet area had been forest" (Thurner 1). What a changed picture could be seen in 1910! This was the "gold rush" of the Upper Peninsula. The bulging population gave testimony to the popularity of Calumet.

Crossing the streets of Calumet were women shopping from store to store and horses pulling carts; in winter, dogs pulled sleds, people wore snowshoes, and sleighs swooshed by. A stagecoach even came through town. "The type of stage used has been described as 'fashioned after the western coaches.' It was a closed carriage with doors on either side, glass panels, and two seats inside facing each other. There were no springs, baggage was loaded on top the coach, and the driver sat 'on a high seat on the outside.' Four horses pulled the stage" (Thurner 11). Traveling through the area were people of several ethnicities. Among these diverse residents of Houghton County were 7,241 Finns (Thurner 13). And among them were the children, Einard and Sophie, unknown to each other, who later met and settled in Gratiot Location where Einard would then work the copper mines for nearly forty years.

People of other European ethnicities in the area—the Austrians, Italians, Germans, Irish, and Poles—saw the Finns as "members of the lowest social strata, a strange breed of solemn, hardworking people, stubborn and peculiar" (Thurner 18). Large families were common, European ethnic diversity in the schools was prevalent, and unique foods were specialties originating from many different backgrounds. Miners commonly carried the famous Upper Peninsula pasty (pronounced "pass-tee") in their tin pails underground. In 1887, the historian Forster "observed them warming drink and pasties later over candles. He described the pasty as 'an enormous turn-over, filled with chopped beefsteak, boiled potatoes and onions with spice.' This 'strong dish' he found 'immensely satisfying' but he warned against eating it at a late hour lest one be haunted by terrifying dreams!" (qtd. in Thurner 31). Einard was among the hard-working laborers that entered the mineshafts faithfully day after day. The hours were very long and the pay was low. The men would awake in the dark, descend the shafts in the dark, work in the dark, and come up out of the shafts in the dark. It was for this reason that they had to rotate shifts or else they would have never seen daylight except on weekends. Every mining family lived with the possibility of sudden disaster. Les recalls days in school when he would hear the air blast vibrating the whole area from an underground explosion in a mine announcing some emergency and the students would wonder whose father had been killed that day. "A 1907 report gave the [high] rate as 10.12 deaths per 1000 men employed in Iron County [for that year]" (Thurner 38). Death became a way of life.

What made conditions worse was that accidents could happen from tumbling rocks or men falling down dark unlit shafts. Young boys worked the mines as well. "Sanitary conditions underground were crude. Empty powder and candle boxes served as latrines [...] in some mines lime was used to dispose of waste [...]. Life was raw" (Thurner 40). To complicate matters, the miners were heavy drinkers and brawlers. One mining location was known as Helltown. "In August, 1919, the situation became so serious that the good people of Helltown (officially called such by the newspapers) were forced to petition their supervisor to take action to stop the lawlessness. Many of the old residents still remember when Helltown was a personification of the wild West, and it was not uncommon to read of several men being badly beaten each night." (Monette 38) Many of the mining "locations" where miners rented and leased homes became the paradise for the drunk and the disorderly.

Gratiot Location was no exception to this where Einard and Sophie settled.

Despite the "world of beer," several Finnish women actually made an effort to have a temperance movement from 1908–1919 (Thurner 64). However, the drinkers seemed to be winning out because churches reported the nuisance of hearing drunks on Sunday morning. Most bars were open from six in the morning until eleven at night. But the Salvation Army ladies did not stop making their rounds to the saloons. "With zither and other musical instruments, they paused at the doors and sang inspirational songs as the men listened, applauded, and sometimes asked for encores" (Thurner 64).

While the miners drank, the company owners were raking in the money. Several sources say that the shops in Calumet did businesses of fifteen to twenty-five thousand dollars per month. What wealth there was in the "Queen City of the North" (Thurner Preface). But strikes and other worlds promising wealth drew people elsewhere and copper mining continued, so the population dropped significantly in Calumet by the 1920's. "In just about a century, Calumet had emerged, flourished, and then retreated" (Thurner 105). A *Mining Gazette* article summed it all up putting its finger on Calumet's strength—her heritage: "Keweenaw County has become well established as a summer retreat for tourists, but a major problem remains in the need to add to year-round strength. Just what is Calumet's stalwart heritage in this time of economic new frontiers? It has been said of turmoil in a community that what is needed to prevent it is to know one another: 'When we know one another, we can live together more peacefully.' Calumet's strength lies there. It is above all a community. Community is not uniformity or adherence to a core of beliefs, but a living entity composed of individuals who may disagree on many issues and whose attitudes may be diametrically opposed. Community is formed by a group of people who find a kind of fulfillment together. Though many at Calumet may not consciously be aware of a sense of community, the sense of belonging despite frictions and misunderstandings bound an ethnic diversity in one conglomerate for many years. The blending of cultures through intermarriage, business associations, schools, work in the mines, social activities, and common joys and sorrows created bonds of belonging that persist for many no matter how far they travel or how their experiences diverge. Despite diversity Calumet seems to have created that rare and sought-after quality of community where one belongs because common experiences of work aspirations, sorrow, and joy transcend ethnicity, religion, and class. Never realized completely, this community existed—and exists. This is Calumet" (Thurner 107).

Einard mined shafts in the Keweenaw that were the deepest in the world. There was no richer copper concentration. It was said that the copper was so pure that it could be used from the ground without being processed. While he would go off to the mine, Sophie ran the house in Gratiot Location. She cooked on a big wood stove in a small kitchen. She hauled the water for the clothes washing and cleaning. It was in this little house outside of the Mohawk Village that Sophie birthed her nine children.

One day an agent came by to get the names of all the kids for the insurance policy for the mining company where Einard worked. Well, Einard said, "There's Gucko Girl, Ron Boy, Beppoo Girl, Stuggler, Heine (pronounced "Hee-nee") or Honey Boy, Dorothy Girl, Mucko Boy, and Sluggo; will that do?" The agent stood wide-eyed and speechless. Einard had nicknames for them all; and after awhile, who knew their real names?

Edward Ollila was Einard and Sophie's first child who died as a baby due to pneumonia. Elaine was then the next child, and she lived in Gratiot until she was sixteen when she left to go to Detroit to work. Ron was born the third and he enlisted in the military at a "younger than permissible" age. Beatrice was the next and she stayed in Gratiot until she later worked in Detroit and lived with her sister, Elaine. Stan was next; he was shot and paralyzed in a hunting accident when he was sixteen, and he lived much of his shortened life in different institutions. Then Heine, his real name Ervin, came along. He was a massive hunk of humanity, a gentle giant who also loved a good laugh. He stayed at the home until he entered the military as well.

Dorothy was the next girl to come along. She was closer in age to the younger two, so they did much together. She ended up leaving and settling out in Colorado when she was in her teens. Earl was born at the Gratiot house not too long after Dorothy. Finally, one day, at the house in Gratiot, with Mrs. Prittig as the midwife, and with the bed moved to the living room once again, the other siblings waited in the kitchen until from behind closed doors in the modest room they heard the cries of Leslie John Ollila, born March 22, 1943. This rough environment framed much of the story for the life of that young child.

Chapter Three
Rugged Finns and Saunas

Nothing of worth comes easy.

— Dr. Les Ollila

Les was a very shy boy, and to compound things, he had a speech impediment that caused him to slur all of his words together. People made fun of Les when he talked so that made him withdraw even more. "I remember when we were kids in Gratiot; the people would come up to Gratiot and we would hide in the bush," Earl said. People would drive up to Gratiot out of curiosity because it was known as the roughest neighborhood in Copper Country. The neighbors were heavy drinkers who carried an arsenal of guns. Not even the county sheriff would come up to Gratiot Location without state police back up. And the state police station was fifty miles away. According to Les, the sheriff insisted on armed protection and reinforcements.

Since Les and Earl were close in age and most of the older siblings had left home to find jobs or to go into the military, many of Les's childhood memories were the things that he and Earl did together. They had to walk from the Gratiot Road to the main road to catch the bus to school; they used to trudge down to the end of the road very early in the morning. By the side of the road, they would use their feet to beat down roadside trails in the deep snow to pretend they were P-17 or P-18's, the big Keweenaw plows.

Earl declared, “Ma bought Les one of the grader trucks one time from Foley’s store in Mohawk. The toy truck had an under blade. And I envied that toy so much that I used to sneak and play with that every chance I got.” The Ollila children never received many big gifts like that, especially in their younger years. After a few more years of their dad working in the mines, Ollilas were able to make a bit more money and get presents from time to time.

The children remember raising chickens in the house that Einard purchased next to theirs in Gratiot Location. Hundreds of chickens filled the adjacent house. Beatrice would walk to the Mohawk post office after school and she heard the chicks peeping in the mailroom ready to be taken home. At home, the chickens filled the upstairs, the downstairs, the basement, and even in the kitchen—all over the place. Einard would get up Saturdays to remind the kids to clean out the chicken “coop” which was really the house next door. Afterwards, they delivered eggs to Mohawk. People would save their egg cartons; so Les, Earl, and Dorothy would ride in the back of an old 1932 Plymouth surrounded by cartons of eggs. They wanted to go to certain customers who gave tips. “If you got a nickel, you were really happy,” Earl reported. This all had to be accomplished on Saturday because Einard could just be planning one of his unusual outings on Sunday.

The feed for the chickens came in sacks and the sacks were a bright-colored cotton fabric; so when the sack was empty, Sophie would take it and wash it and cut it into a pattern and make dresses for Beatrice and Dorothy. Dorothy and Beatrice would lie down in the back of the '32 Plymouth when they drove through Mohawk because they were afraid their friends would see them in their dresses made from the sacks for chicken mash.

After the chicken coop was cleaned, Dad Ollila planned a trip to Eagle Harbor to pick blueberries. These were the best memories that any of the children have. Beatrice recalls that on the way to *and* the way home from these blueberry picking expeditions, they were able to stop and get ice cream which was such a treat to anticipate. When they would arrive in Eagle Harbor, they would get a huge wooden bucket out of the back of the car and each child carried his or her own pail as well. The Ollila children had to fill those pails and that big bucket full of berries before they could go swimming. Ron remembers: "It was about four or five in the evening when all the black flies were out; they were biting us. We swam and we had hot dogs." A grown Les saved that big blueberry bucket to remind himself of the good days when they would picnic together as a family. Les holds onto this memory as one of a few precious moments.

Also in the summertime, Earl and Les would play ball on Gratiot Road that wound up past the sawmill and the copper mine. Earl explains: "You took a baseball; if you needed to put a cover on it you took some friction tape and put that on it. Or we would play with a golf ball. I never knew why they were there, but we had golf balls. Ron used to be a caddy up there in Copper Harbor so we must have gotten them from him." The brothers had to make do with what they had.

Since the copper mine was located next to Gratiot Location, the rock piles that surrounded the mine would get high. In the wintertime, the boys would take the wax-covered dynamite boxes that the miners threw into the garbage and make them into sleds and then slide them on a trail down the rock pile. Or they would use boards, barrel boards, and then nail them together; and they would sit on the slick board sled and slide down the hill. Dorothy, Earl, and Les would go to the rock pile on rare days off from school. A big steam plant was built where the miners ran a winch to cable the cars. The kids climbed in back of the steam plant; and when that steam was operating the winch, there was a big pipe that came out the back; and when the steam was released, it would blow from the pipe and they stood nearby and warmed up. The youngsters never realized that they were also getting soaking wet. Back home, Ma Ollila ritually made pasties. She also made traditional *rieska*, round bread. When they returned cold and wet from the rock piles, that warm bread and creamed farm butter would greet them. They smothered their bread with homemade thimbleberry jam, too.

Heine (or Ervin), Les's older brother, was a father figure to Les. Their grandfather, who had a special love for Heine, called Heine *Honey Boy*. Somehow Honey Boy became the nickname Heine. He was a massive, strong young man. He was musical, too, playing guitar to rival the best from Tennessee. He also tinkered with cars. In the 1950's, he had a mint 1932 Chrysler, probably purchased from a farmer somewhere. Earl remembered that car well: "It had a straight six engine in it. And Heine went to Eagle Harbor one night with his buddies and they were drinking and the car stalled or they ran out of gas and they left it by the side of the road. Somebody took a pipe and rammed a hole through the radiator and the roof." Heine fixed the radiator leak eventually, but he took the roof from the doghouse and set that on top of the car and left it there so the car roof wouldn't leak. Heine also lifted weights and Earl and Les would join him. If they dared lie down for a break, Heine would give them a swat on the head and tell them to get movin.'

Hard work was the name of the game growing up. Earl and Les had to saw wood with a bent, steel handled saw for the household's heating and cooking. They used to go and cut the dry wood out of the bush and drag those long logs home and pile them. They had to cut them to stove-length by hand. The older boys were gone, so that responsibility fell on Earl and Les when they were still not yet teens. Their dad would cut wood from down the road and the boys had to take the *gelka* sled as they called it—they had Finnish names for everything—and load it up with wood and drag it home and throw the wood in a pile.

As was typical for that area, the Gratiot Location home had an outhouse. Les and Earl remember well: "We used to have an outdoor toilet and if we had to go to the bathroom in the winter time, we would have a pail in the hallway upstairs and there would be a box over the top; it was an old orange crate. We used to have to take turns hauling the slop pail out—we called it a slop pail." They had to take it out to the outhouse and dump it and they had to be sure not to splash any on the toilet seat. Les and Earl never remember having regular toilet paper. The substitute was the JC Penney catalog, Wards, or Sears.

Ma Ollila's life was washing clothes or preparing food. She would scrub the clothes by hand, including Einard's mining clothes that had to be washed separately, and she would hang them out on the line. In the wintertime, the snow was so high that the bottoms of the clothes were just hanging in the snow. The work clothes stood like frozen statues. The boys used to get these frozen clothes off the line and carry them in the house all the way upstairs climbing up into the third floor. No one could stand completely straight up in what was really the attic. There was a clothesline up in the attic where Ma would hang the clean clothes until they thawed. She never complained—it was all she knew.

Einard was a heavy smoker. He never smoked brand name cigarettes—"tailor-mades" as Les called them. So Les and Earl used a rolling machine to make cigarettes for their dad. This was routine life for these Gratiot Location boys.

Also, Ma Ollila used to bottle deer meat—the family ate venison. At Grandpa Ollila's farm, towards Eagle River, about two miles down the road from Grandpa's place, there was another road that went to a little mine. In the summertime when the family needed the meat, Einard and the boys would go to that spot with a flashlight. Those times stick out in the boys' memories: "Dad would have the gun and we'd drive in there and sit and be real quiet and then when you could see some movement in the apple trees, then you put the flashlight on them and 'Boom!' dad would shoot the deer and we would have some meat." They had to get their meat that way; it made the most sense. Ma canned the meat because owning a freezer was unheard of for them.

"Dad would pick thimbleberries until they were coming out of Ma's ears. She'd get in the kitchen in the hot summer time, cooking them on the hot stove in that little kitchen. She would cook them up, and she said at one point, 'When are you going to stop picking these thimbleberries?' and he looked at her and said, 'I pick the berries woman; you boil them,'" is what the boys recall. That was the end of the discussion. Then Les, Dorothy, and Earl would sell the jars of thimbleberries by the side of the road. They sold fresh strawberries as well as thimbleberries, blackberries, boysenberries—anything to add to the family income.

When Les was still just a boy, he and Ron were once riding together in one of Ron's trucks used for hauling logs. They were coming up a hill by Malilas and Ron went to shift gears and the throttle rod jumped off and the motor died out and he had a huge load of logs; and the truck started rolling down the hill. At first, Ron backed it into a snow bank. There was a guy operating a bulldozer, so Les ran up the hill and called to that guy and the driver came down and they hooked a cable on the front of the truck. He started pulling, and all of a sudden, he released the winch and the cable let go and here the truck was rolling back down the hill again. While Ron was trying to control the load of logs before they dumped and little Les was trying to hold on to the brake, the bulldozer driver locked his gears and the cable went taut and the bulldozer when up straight and it almost dumped over backwards. Then the driver released it again and here was little Les holding onto the brake while Ron was trying to crawl under the rig to hook the throttle back up. It's a miracle that they survived. Les's training in the driving and operation of huge trucks and equipment began in his boyhood days.

Ron enlisted in the army when he was only sixteen, but Einard didn't know where he was. Two weeks later he asked Sophie, "Where's Ronald Boy?" And she said, "Oh, he's in the army." "In the army? How in the world did he get there?" (One can see the close-knit family that they were.) "There was no comradery with sports or anything. We wanted to play baseball. Baseball nothing!—Go out and get some more wood!" is what the fellows heard. Life was rugged and as Einard would say, "Quit that monkey-shinin'!"

The boys learned to hunt and fish, and they adapted to the outdoors. Their dad would trap beaver or otter or weasels and this was not only a time to be with dad, but the Ollila sons all turned out to be capable guides for hunting and trapping. They used to take the animals and cut around the nose and pull the skin off of the carcass and then peel it inside out and push a flat board inside that hide. Once they stretched it out, then they took a knife and scraped all the rest of the hide and cleaned it really well. When it dried, they could take it to the DNR officer who gave them so much money for a weasel and so much for a mink and so much for a beaver. Earl related, "I remember going trapping with the snow shoes strapped on our backs—we would go in the springtime on the hard snow without sinking. One time we caught five beaver in those traps." They took a long time coming out of the woods because it was now mid-afternoon and the snow was no longer hard. Those beaver were heavy—sixty pounds each. After they got the animals out of the woods, they lugged them home and skinned them. The cheapest part of the hide was the belly where the skin was the thinnest. They didn't want to damage the back because that is what they made coats of and other products. They would stretch the hides with the tacks or nails on the board, and they kept stretching them until they were to the maximum size. Einard stacked the pelts and made the money from them.

In the spring, Heine would go into the bush when the coyotes would have their pups. Eventually, he could find their tracks in the snow. If he found the tracks, he could follow them backwards to the den. Heine had a real knack for that. He would retrace the trail and find a secondary hole. He would go in making sure the mother wasn't there, pull pups out, load them in a gunny sack, and take them to the DNR who would pay him for the young coyotes. Since coyotes would eat all the rabbits and chase all of the deer, the DNR was glad to get the pups to dispose of them.

It cannot be overstated that drinking was a major problem always serving as a background in the neighborhood. Drunks sometimes ended up in a "boarding" house that they called "The Japanese Embassy" because the inhabitants had a Japanese flag outside on a large limb. It was a shack back in the woods and several of these men that hung out there were WWII vets who had risked their lives to fight for the country, but alcohol was a debilitating problem for many of them. Marty Von visited the "embassy" one time with Les when Marty and Les were in their thirties. Marty shares the following:

We got there at night and knocked on the door. There was no answer so Dr. O checked the door to see if it was open; and when we opened the door and went in, it's like heads appeared from every corner of the room. It was like one huge room—one huge bunkhouse. It seemed like there were dozens of beds there and people would lift up their heads and here they were drunk and could hardly communicate, but they were always happy to see Les.

This was the environment that Les was exposed to all of his life growing up. The men were very kind to Les and Marty, but they would say the funniest things. One guy rubbed another guy's head while calling him Napoleon. A couple of them got into an argument that Les was the strongest man in the UP and he could arm wrestle them all and win. The men basically took their welfare checks and went and spent the cash on booze; then they would borrow and pawn everything else to drink. The Ollila brothers, Les and Earl, learned to cope with such hardship with laughter. They could have chosen bitterness, but they chose humor.

Gratiot was not the nice neat little American town. Typically, Les and Earl would get up and go over daily to visit a neighbor. He would firmly remind the young men that he didn't have a driver's license because he lost it years ago because of drinking and driving. He would pretend that they were going to dig in the dump for a while to find stuff. In reality, this man's intention was to get drunk eventually.

So Earl and Les would take these neighbors to the bars—*Bucket of Blood* first—in Mohawk, or they would stop at *The White House* bar. The boys would sit in the car and wait for them to come out. Then they would go to *Copper City Bar* and then sometimes up to Calumet on 5th Street to another bar. Les was sitting in the car one time. It was just Les and Reino this time. Reino Maki was in the bar and he was drunk; he was a big man and he liked to arm wrestle, and one time he decided to brag about his friend, Les. He said that he had somebody in the car that can beat anybody in the bar. Reino came out "wide-stepping" it as they say, and he insisted that Les come in and show his strength. Reino said, "Wes, [instead of "Les"] come on in there and arm wrestle these bums." Les managed to get Reino back into the car and back out of town.

A school pal of Les's was a guy by the name of Jack Spreitzer. Connie Parski was Jack's mom, but she was Wilfred Maki's common law wife. Wilfred was epileptic, so when he drank, the fits were compounded. Something was always stirring in Gratiot, but one night, life changed drastically for Jack while Les was there to witness it. Everyone was home at Gratiot this one particular evening when Les's family heard racket coming from across the street. Wilfred, in one of his drunken, epileptic seizures beat Connie to death. When Les's mother approached the street, she said she saw Wilfred dragging Connie by the hair through the street and the family remembers her head bobbing up and down on the rocks of the road. She was dead and Les's mother watched Wilfred drag her down to the dump and throw her in. Les found Connie in the dump, and Earl ran to the Gratiot mine late at night to use the phone to report the murder. It was the nearest phone, and the night shifts made it possible to use that phone in emergency. Jack sat across from the courthouse when Wilfred went to trial, and Jack was determined to shoot the murderer if he got a chance. Thankfully, he never did. Meanwhile, Les encouraged Jack during these difficult days and helped his friend walk through this traumatic event without seeing Jack fall apart because of his loss.

Les was terribly shy in high school, but Earl and Les were star athletes for the Calumet High School football and track teams. Einard was all about cleaning out chicken coops, chopping wood, and carrying water. Sports in high school were not the focus for Einard and his bonding with the boys. He was just a hard working man. Earl was a first team running back and Les was the fullback. That particular year they had not lost any games. Somebody from the mines asked their dad if he was going to see his boys play. Einard really didn't even know what football was all about. The guy from work convinced him to go one night. So he went up to Agassi field and watched a game one time. The announcer kept saying, "Ollila goes for so many yards, or Ollila does this or that!" Einard looked at somebody next to him and said, "Why are they gabbing Ollila this or that?" He left after the game never to attend another.

Les and Earl used to bring one towel into the locker room. When they could stand it up in a corner, they thought that it was about time to bring it home to wash. The boys had to hitchhike home after track or football practice. In their early teens, they had no car and they hitchhiked or walked until they could get their own cars. It was a seven-mile walk—a long hike after a long practice. Les did not own fancy sneakers and he remembers playing junior high football in work boots. In fact, Les would run on the beaches of Lake Superior in the work boots to build his leg strength and stamina.

When Earl graduated from high school, he was all dressed up to go to the baccalaureate ceremony. He remembers, "Our dog got loose. It was out in the bush and I chased after that dog and I finally caught it in a bush. Because I was dressed up, my dad says, 'Where are you goin?' And I said to baccalaureate." Laurium was a town east of Calumet causing Einard to respond this way: "What in the world is in the *back of Laurium*?" "What's going on back there?" Baccalaureate? Back of Laurium? Such was the rugged Finnish wit. Earl just accepted it and his dad's lack of understanding and went to the baccalaureate alone.

Brother Stanley had been shot in a hunting accident up north when he was sixteen years old, leaving him paralyzed from the waist down. He was on crutches, but he received accounting training and he worked as an accountant in offices later on. When forty-nine, Stanley was close to death at the Newberry Hospital, but Les was the key guy, the one who took on responsibility, and diligently saw to Stanley's needs. Les was the key guy in Heine's life, too. They had special relationships. Heine would listen to Les. Heine and Stan both struggled with drinking, but Les was always there to help and rebuke them. Les would tell Heine what to do and scold him and Heine would agree that was what he should do. Les took the bulk of responsibility of following up on all of Heine's activities; and after Heine died, Les had mountains of work to sort out from the legal mess that Heine left behind in Gratiot. Heine was a soft touch, so he would buy just about anything from his neighbors to give them spending money. He even bought their houses in Gratiot Location. Les had to pick through piles of trash to find paperwork to settle his brother and family's estate. Heine had lived out his days in the Gratiot home after Einard and Sophie went to live on Elaine's farm. The old house where Heine had lived had at least twenty televisions that Heine must have lent money for, and he ended up holding onto them.

Einard retired from the mines after thirty-eight years, and he ended up with a dollar a year retirement fund and he had to fight for that. Einard was one of the best miners in the UP. He could get more company count in copper than anyone else. One day after he had retired, he was off trapping beaver. He trudged with a sixty-pound beaver on his back for miles on his way home. He dropped the beaver in the shed and he said, "Fill me a cup of coffee, Mama." And he fell flat on the floor. He had a stroke there and then. He was never the same. Despite the rough home life and sometimes-tumultuous marriage that Einard and Sophie had, they stuck it out together and she took care of her husband following his stroke.

Les says that he got his Ritalin from the tip of his dad's mining boot and from the buckle of his dad's belt. A child stepped out of line once in the Ollila home, and he never tried it again. His dad taught them all the value of hard work and obedience. They didn't do anything for themselves until everything around home that needed to be done was finished. Les has never one time complained about his rugged Finnish background. Instead, he has turned what could be bitter memories into times of recounting humorous incidences from the past spent in the unusual location called *Gratiot*.

The Finnish Sauna—a must!

No story about a Finn would be complete without mentioning the significance of the sauna. One could do an entire study on the sauna; and, in fact, entire books have been written on the phenomenon. The Ollila family's affinity for the sauna was no exception. The Finns used to build the sauna before they built the house or even before they built the barn. And then they lived in the sauna while they built the house and barn. Finnish colonists brought the sauna to Michigan and other states in the 1880s and 1890s.

"Sauna" is a Finnish word for bathhouse. "It is natural for Americans to pronounce it 'sawna,' to rhyme [...] with fauna, but the word should really have an 'ow' sound, as in 'How now brown sauna?' In a phonetic language such as Finnish, every letter is sounded, including the 'u' in 'sauna'" (Hillila 7). The idea of the sauna is one of entering this atmosphere of intense heat experiencing cleansing and drug-free relaxation.

The sauna is truly a way of life. In Finland the saunas can be found in the backyards of almost every home, in apartments, in college dormitories, in hotels, in factories, and many summer homes along lakes (Star 1). Friends and families gather in the dry heat with an occasional burst of steam. It can be a time of conversation, or just a time of grunting and listening to nonsense talk. "Finnish businessmen, says one of the many books on the subject, delight in taking 'their adversaries' to the sauna. Hostility melts in the steam as [...] stubborn minds begin to accept compromise. Rank and protocol are shed in the dressing room with one's clothes, and it is hard to maintain pompous dignity in a birthday suit" (Star 1). Maybe hostile businessmen are convinced to change their ways because temperatures can rise to 175-210 degrees.

The heating is accomplished "by a *kiuas* (pronounced "cue us"), which is a heating unit covered with stones. The stones are heated until super hot [...]. The relative humidity is increased by throwing small amounts of water on the *kiuas*. However, the air remains comparatively dry, because much of the moisture is absorbed by the wooden walls, ceiling, and shelves" (Hillila 8). Besides acting as the family cleansing agent, the Finns would cure meat in the sauna, work leather, have babies, and prepare brides. The saunas have bleachers made of wood and they are graded in height. The lower the bleacher, the lower the temperature. That way everyone may choose a bleacher for maximum enjoyment. "There are no ministers, VIP's, laborers, or lumberjacks on the sauna platform, only sauna mates" sitting naked and truly stripped bare of pretense (Hillila 37).

As the Ollilas grew, they never had a bath in the house. On Saturday, summer and winter, they used to go to Raisanan Sauna in Fulton, Dineys Sauna in Mohawk, Jukkuri's Sauna in Laurium, or the one in Calumet on Pine Street. That was an every Saturday night tradition. Their motto was the following: "Sit on the lower bankie [bench] and you can breath." To get in the sauna was twenty-five cents. All the boys would pile in. There was a bucket of cold water and pop for a nickel, but most of the time they could just drool because they couldn't afford the pop. These saunas had a stove that they heated up in the morning and the rocks got good and hot. When the coals were red hot, they would stick the lunka across the chimney and a piece of metal that they slid through the chimney and they'd block the heat from going out of the sauna. Those great big Finns from Mohawk and Fulton were in the sauna, and their goal was to steam everyone else out.

After the sauna, they took a pail of water or bucket with ice water and dumped it over their heads. It would close all of the body's pores. However, the Ollila boys used to go out in the deep UP snow banks behind the saunas, wearing no clothing, and fall back on the cold snow to make snow angels. To this day, Les will take men into the sauna in their Dunbar home and induct them into the "Finnish Sauna Counseling Center."

Les's love for his fellow Finns and his genuine concern for neighbors and friends supersede his temptation to run from his upbringing. It also supersedes the temptation to pity himself for the circumstances that he endured as a child. He relishes the good times and recalls the humorous stories that he can now rehearse for anyone who will listen. He enjoys sitting in a room with a group of friends, and the laughter will endure for hours as he rolls along non-stop sharing the funny Finnish ways.

CHAPTER FOUR
THE HART HOTEL

People will be your greatest source of blessing.

— Dr. Les Ollila

The sound that was most keenly familiar to Les and Earl was the crunching of gravel as the old blue Plymouth station wagon drove slowly up the road to Gratiot Location. Les says often that if it weren't for the man that drove that old blue Plymouth that Les would be in an alcoholic grave right now. Pastor Charles Hart decided in his ministry as the pastor of First Baptist Church in Calumet, that he was going to love young people and pour his life into theirs. It was not something that he specifically planned out in his mind and heart, but it was something that came naturally for Reverend Hart.

The church had a series of evangelistic meetings with Phil Ward, a former gangster, and two of the young girls from the church had just moved out to Mohawk; the girls wanted to invite some of the people from the area out to church. Les, Earl, and Jimmy Hill and a number of their buddies came. As a result of the meetings, several of the boys asked Jesus Christ to come into their hearts and be their Savior because of the testimony of Phil Ward who had been converted himself. Les made a profession because his pals did. Pastor Hart remembers meeting Les for the first time: "That's how I came to know Les at that time, you see.

Les didn't have a way into church; he couldn't drive; he was only ten years old." Pastor Hart went back and picked the boys up on Sunday night for a service and on Wednesday night for the prayer service as well. And from then on began a wonderful, deep relationship of love and fellowship as the doors of the Hart home were opened to the Ollila boys, and the Hart's home became theirs. The Ollila boys christened the Hart's house, The Hart Hotel.

Mrs. Joyce Hart's father started the Gitche Gumee Bible Camp in Eagle River, Michigan, in the Upper Peninsula. Joyce spent her summers up at camp helping her dad with all sorts of groups of families and teens that attended. One summer, after the programs were printed, she noticed one phrase—*This young, enthusiastic song leader*. Mrs. Hart, then Miss Joyce Rader, was sixteen at the time. She said that description of that song leader really caught her eye. She recalls, "The description didn't say handsome, but he was that, too." Pastor Hart was twenty-two and even though Miss Rader was sixteen, she was worth waiting for. They married when she was nineteen and have remained so for a glorious sixty-plus years together in ministry.

Pastor Hart drove Les and Earl to church every week until they were old enough to drive themselves. Sometimes a church bus would come out as well and drive young people in for activities. On Sundays especially, Gratiot was rather quiet because everyone was sleeping off his or her binges from the night before. From the time Les was ten years old, he and Earl really enjoyed being around the Hart family. They actually became like sons to Pastor Hart and he became a father figure to them. The Harts had five children of their own—Carol, Lois, Patty, Ginger, and Jack—and these five considered Les and Earl their very own brothers, too.

Les was so shy, but he would go to help Pastor Hart at camp when Les was just a young boy. He worked out at Gitche Gumee until people began showing up, and then he would want to leave because he didn't want to be around people. He had a lisp and it made him extremely self-conscious. Les worked on digging ditches, cutting trees, running errands—anything he could do to help. He also worked with one of the Makis, neighbors from Gratiot, on building chimneys and fireplaces at the camp. This also began a relationship that Les treasures uniting him with the camping ministry and its potential to change the lives of children, teens, and families.

Pastor Hart is a godly, saintly man—he mentored the two Ollilas and many other neighborhood young people, took them out to the woods, had them build things, and just made himself their friend. He was humorous; he was fun to be with—always gentle, and those guys really looked up to him as a dad. He would play hockey with the boys, and he became totally involved in his investment in their lives—it was wonderful—they were caring for the children's needs because Les and Earl's parents could not always meet those needs. While Einard and Sophie provided for the family a home and shelter, the Harts provided a haven of fun and fellowship.

After school, many a day, the boys would make their way over to the Hart's house. Some days they fell asleep right on the living room floor by the fire, and other days they filled the house with laughter. The Hart family loved the down-home spirit of the boys. They made themselves at home by raiding the refrigerator or flopping down on the carpet to snooze. The Hart children and the Ollila boys all grew up together. Lois and Carol Hart were the ones closest in age, so they were all part of one big youth group of twenty-five to thirty Calumet area youth. Pastor Hart drove great distances to pick up teens from Houghton-Hancock all the way up to Copper Harbor. Carol (Hart) Kersey relates, "Les and Earl were the essence of what the UP [Upper Peninsula] culture was. If we could take Andy Griffith out of Mayberry, you wouldn't have Mayberry. If you took Les and Earl out of Calumet, it wouldn't have been the same." Les and Earl would come over to the Harts and mimic the town folk by repeating funny sayings or unique idiosyncrasies, not in a mocking way, but a fun way. They could get laughter out of Pastor Hart like no others could.

For instance, Les and Earl would imitate the Finns at the village saunas. While sitting around, waiting for a sauna stall to become available, the sauna-goers would tell stories and rehearse the events of the week. The typical pose as they conversed would be head down, arms and legs crossed, upper foot flexing up and down. If there was a lull in the conversation, they would fill any awkward silence by uttering, "Yuh…Yuh…," sometimes drawing out the word, sometimes repeating it in quick succession, affirming what the others had said. Les and Earl's comic imitation of this sauna communication entertained the entire Hart household.

About the time that the Catholic Church was deciding on the next pope, the boys decided that Pastor Hart would make a good pope, so they started calling him "The Pope." "We are going to Popey's house," they would say. They loved him dearly. And that was their love language to say, "This is the guy we really love." They were an integral part of the Hart's routine. The gang of young people would pour into Hart's home after church on Sunday night. Or they'd come in on Wednesday—or after ball games. And at Christmas time they would come—and so on.

"Big name youth workers" that led rallies and conferences did not come that far north, so the group decided that they would make their own fun and draw in other youth. They were constantly creating entertainment, and Les and Earl were the ringleaders. Carol (Hart) Kersey and Lois Hart remember Christmases especially:

> *When Christmas vacation arrived, there would be crowds at our house every night. We'd listen to Christmas music, play games, or just talk and tell*

stories. Sometimes we would get out the old reel-to-reel tape recorder and read funny skits from one of Dad's books, passing around the microphone while we acted out our particular character, laughing and making fun of each other as we read. One memorable melodrama we recorded ended with the heroine sighing, "My hero!" in such a funny way that the phrase often emerged in conversation later and became the title of the skit in our minds.

Another thing that the young people would do is to gather around the piano and to sing in harmony through a hymnal, the old gospel songs like "On the Jericho Road." They would pump out the activities hour after hour, having fun and never being bored.

Mrs. Hart always hovered around the kitchen fixing what little she had but multiplying it constantly for all who filled her home. Rarely did Pastor Hart ever say that anyone had to go home. The truth is that he didn't want to miss the action, and Les and Earl made him laugh. He loved them as his own. After eating, they would get a rhythm game going. Each person was assigned a number. In unison around the living room, the young people tapped their knees, clapped their hands, and then snapped their fingers to keep the rhythm going without missing a beat. After the first snap, one person would say his own number and then call out someone else's number. The rhythm would go faster and faster until someone messed up the numbering. When that person blew it, the room erupted in laughter. They never had to have anything special to do—just as long as they could have fun and laugh like crazy.

Les and Earl made things humorous even though some times in their lives could have been painful. It may have been the way that they endured personal pain. They'd put their twist on it and the whole group would break up in laughter. Some things were distinctively Les, but always in the context of the Upper Peninsula culture. He imitated people so well. He'd draw you in and make you feel that you were witnessing whatever it was. You could envision these crazy people in various locations. Some of them were "touched." Les was never bitter—he dealt with his upbringing with humor.

Mrs. Hart was the epitome of patience. Since she was busy in the kitchen getting food prepared—baking sweets and cooking hot dishes—food never ran out. The Harts were never in their life a wealthy family, but they gave what they could share. The Hart table was often full as the teens laughed and ate and shared unforgettable moments together. What the boys didn't realize either was that the Harts were the janitors at the church, the snow shovelers, the fire starters in the furnace, the bus drivers, parents of five of their own, and yet surrogate parents to many children from Gratiot Location without so much as one time making the kids feel unwelcome in the church or in their home.

Gratiot Location sat in the Keweenaw Peninsula that was surrounded by water with Lake Superior wrapping its way all around the Copper Country. Many times, the teens decided to go to the beach, sit around, sing, talk, or just have fun. Eagle Harbor beach was a popular spot. In particular in Eagle Harbor, one very important aspect of the Calumet high school student gatherings was the infamous Bear Pits. Many a famous circus would have hired Les and Earl or Jimmy Hill for their ring master talents. The big attraction in town was to pass the word that everyone would meet at the Bear Pit at a particular time. All the vehicles with their brave occupants would pull up to the Bear Pit quietly as not to spoil the environment (spook the bears). There was protocol for this ritual. Headlights were extinguished and everyone would wait in hushed silence, as indeed, the bear would appear. The Bear Pits were, in reality, the local dumps. No one dared open windows because the smell would suffocate the spectators in their cars. But Les and Earl would pretend that they had microphones for vast audiences from as far away as Ohio. They were the MC's for the evening of Bear Pit viewing. "The brown bears are brown and the black bears are black," they would proclaim. "And for you poor folk from Ohio, these bears eat garbage!" Their imagination would go on and on and the MC's for the Bear Pit would give their rendition of information as if they were in the middle of the circus ring entertaining the crowd. Then Les and Earl and Jimmy would pretend that the MC's voice was becoming hoarse, and the bear would begin to come close to the MC. (Of course, the MC's were sitting in the car, still.) All the time pretending, the MC would then have to take his microphone and jump into the trunk of someone's car to avoid being attacked by the mean bear. All of this was make-believe.

Les, Earl, and Jimmy would continue to make up their stories as they went along. They would feed off of each other's ideas and get more elaborate with each minute. They pretended that this job was a coveted position, and they were making a lot of money in this particular profession. This was their version of the drive-in theater on a night when they really needed some entertainment. In actuality, the scene before these teens after an evening at camp Gitche Gumee was in the simplest terms—a dump and bears scrounging for garbage.

When Private First Class Earl Ollila was in Denver, Colorado, a few years later, in September of 1966, he wrote Lois Hart a letter commenting on those "Bear Pit" days. He went into one of his MC Bear spiels. His letter went something like this:

> *I know that my sincere heart has caused some poor soul to rejoice. Ohio people and all [that was always part of the bear speech]—they all come for guidance and instruction, big and small, old and young. I've worked for years and years and I'm sure that you all feel the same, but my work won't*

go unrewarded. I've worked hard and deserve a good word now and then. Even now while the bear season is coming to a close, I've got my next year's program figured out. More speeches and more push on the town people to haul better garbage. Bears are good bears—need good food—need help. I'm just the man to help them. I know and we all know that I'm well-trained in the bears' habits. And need to get better dumps and better garbage. You know this Lady Byrd program to keep the highways clean, well, that's due to a direct request of me. You know, don't throw the garbage on the road but in the dumps. You see that I'm dedicated and well-organized in my work. I had an experience with a lady this summer. She didn't believe that bears were garbage eaters. When she left me, she was more convinced that they were. She was even eating garbage herself. Not the boxes, but the garbage. She had a good head on her. I told her that I had a good paying job, a dollar a day and all I could eat. Well, summer is good, but in winter I starve. I have to go to warm weather to continue my work. Hey, I have to stop now because I have to sleep, too you know. Your guide, Earl.

So those bear pit days became a lifelong joke that tied the teens together.

Other members of the church became very special to the gang from the Hart Hotel. Dave Coltman, their local high school English teacher had an open door policy to his home. Even though Dave himself had lost two children in separate tragic incidents, he reached out to the Ollila boys and other young people with incredible passion and faithfulness. Dave would do things like take a car hood and drag it behind his car in the winter and give the young people rides. Dave would come to ball games and make each of those young people feel special. Dave and Esther would always invite the boys to their home from school to stay Wednesday nights for supper, and then they would all go to the church together.

Besides youth group activities, Earl and Les were star players on the Calumet High School football team. Pastor Hart faithfully attended nearly every one of their games. One football game in particular brings back memories for Charles Hart. Les got injured in the game at Lake Linden, about four miles from Calumet. Earl was the running back and Les was the right halfback; he was doing a lot of blocking, but the ground was slippery. He blocked one time for Earl and slipped, causing Earl to plant his foot right on one of Les's kidneys. Pastor Hart, who was watching, had his station wagon with him at the game. The coach thought that Les should get right to the hospital, so pastor took him. The town was repairing the roads at the time, so it was a rough ride. The station wagon was definitely not made to have a bed in it. The state police escorted the station wagon up the hill with Les inside the vehicle flat on his back. Every bump made Les ache even more. Earl remembers that night for another reason:

> *On the way back from the game, a guy who was the president of GM's son was going to Michigan Tech and he let someone use his Corvette. When you go to Laurium, there is the street that y's together; this guy didn't know that he was supposed to stop there. So he came and he smashed into my 1949 Ford. He smashed the front of the grill in, so I drove it as far as I could before it overheated; and that was between Mohawk and Ahmeek. So I get home finally and Ma says, "Where ya been?" And I says, "I had a little accident," and she says, "You had an accident?" And then she says, "Where's Les?" And I says, "Oh, he's up in Calumet hospital."*

That all took place on the same evening. Since everything happened so quickly, that was the first that their folks even heard that Les was in the hospital. Les and Earl had to fend for themselves many times. This was one of those times.

On Christmas Eve, the young people from the church youth group would pile in a car to go and sing for others who were shut-in, seniors, or those in the hospital. Les was constantly thinking of others—many times charitable ideas were his ideas. It was a gift—a God-given gift. Upon return to the Hart Hotel on Christmas Eve all tired out, Les announced one time, "We were out spreading Christmas cheer, but the spreader broke." Of course, he was referring to the manure spreader just to make everyone laugh once again.

Then there were Christmas mornings—a ritual in the Hart Hotel. Mrs. Hart remembers making an effort to get up extra early on Christmas morning so that her children could open their presents since they knew that the Ollila boys would soon pop in. Pastor and Mrs. Hart and their children always knew that the boys would be coming for certain.

In 1958, a local high school band concert performed in town. The bunch from the youth group went together, and Lois Hart to this day has a copy of the program. They spent their time rewriting the program in Upper Peninsula lingo. For example, the program said that there was a number about Bathsheba. Jack Spreitzer, Les, and Earl scribbled that out and wrote in, "Sauna-sheba." That was their kind of humor—and at the time they were hysterical with laughter. They didn't have TV's, computers, or electronic games—so they created their own fun.

One spring when the smelt were running on the Gratiot River, the "gang" from the Hart Hotel went out and caught buckets of the tiny fish in the middle of the night. Then they went to Gratiot Location to cook them in the wood stove. In the wee hours of the morning, Einard and Sophie were awakened by the smell of the fish in the house and the noisy bunch in the kitchen.

Because the youth group gathered constantly, Lois Hart and Les were each other's first attraction. Lois and Les were considered a pair from junior high through senior high. It was the practice of the local football players, without the coach's approval, to take a cleat from the football shoes, bore a hole in it, and put it on a chain for a girl. Lois received a holey cleat necklace from Les. Lois recalls, "It got tempestuous at times; I suppose due to two strong-willed emerging adults. But we also were great buddies. We had an immediate rapport when we met as kids and got acquainted through our youth group at the church, at camp, and finally on our own as we started dating." One afternoon, Les said, "Goin' town to see Lois." Dad told Earl that they were to stack wood before anything else happened. Les refused. Earl and Les broke out in an all out fistfight in the kitchen. Mom's mop bucket spilled all over them and the floor, and their burly bodies rolled into the wood stove and pushed it across the floor. In the end, Earl was stacking wood, and Les got to go into town.

At Gitche Gumee one summer, toward the end of Lois's high school career, another guy came along in whom Lois was interested. He was on the camp staff. She and Les continued writing even as Les had moved on to Detroit after his graduation, but when it looked like her interests were elsewhere, they discontinued writing. A few months later, Les met Charlene and the rest is "their" history. Lois never regretted their friendship, and it has filled in many memories from the Hart Hotel for her. Upon Les's engagement to Charlene, Les and Lois wrote once more and wished each other God's blessings on their lives. The closure was complete. She writes, "You have heard the saying, 'Less is More.' **Les** was more, too—more than the kid from Gratiot, more than any of us would have guessed at that time. God lay hold of him and used him in surprising ways." Les learned of the open door policy as a result of being one of Hart's sons, and his days at the Hart Hotel would stand him in good stead all the days of his ministry.

CHAPTER FIVE
THE GRATIOT CATS

Never forget how to laugh.

— Dr. Les Ollila

Growing up in Gratiot Location, one had to laugh to survive. The group of local guys that became fast friends were Les and Earl, Jack Spreitzer, Owen Isaacson, the Nowiki brothers, the Hill boys, and a few others who joined in now and then. It is a miracle that any of them are alive today—their antics were often death defying, illegal, or just plain stupid. Their craziness usually centered around the Ollila home located in Gratiot. They still had outdoor toilets in the forties and fifties; they still took the milk to the basement to keep it cool. Town folk looked at these boys as hicks from the bush, so to further agitate the local gossips they gave themselves the name, *The Gratiot Cats.* The group formed over the years and stayed together until some went off to the army, on to college, or on to the big cities like Detroit or Chicago to make money.

Jack Spreitzer lived in Mohawk. His mother had a live-in boyfriend in Gratiot, so he would go out there with her quite a bit. Jack met Les in grade school, and their friendship began. Jimmy Hill was the first to go to church, and the other boys followed when Pastor Hart came up to Gratiot with his station wagon. Jack enjoyed the cookies that the church gave to him. They were all needy boys with troubling family backgrounds including alcoholism, incest, unfaithfulness, and poverty. They bonded and their friendships always ended up in bundles of laughter—they did anything for laughs. Their medicine for their problems was a good joke, a laugh, or a project that they could embark on together as *The Gratiot Cats.*

One time Jack remembers getting Les into some trouble when they were high school age. The week before, Jack had been to the dance hall with some buddies when Rocky Myers and some of the bullies started picking on them. Jack said, "Hey, we'll be back next week." That week he gathered up a bunch of guys to go back. Les didn't know what they were getting into. They all went over to the upstairs teen center hall in Hancock and some pushing and shoving started. Les turned to leave wanting no part of the fight, but the other rebels blocked the stairwell. Les decided to give them the "cross-armed shove," and they all tumbled down the stairs. Running to Jack, Les said, "What in the world is going on?" He didn't have a clue what was up. They left along with the bullies and the fight was avoided. But Les wasn't very happy that Jack had duped him into an unexpected fight. Jack thought Les would take a swing at him—when Les got angry, he would swing at something. That's where he got his nickname, Sluggo. Jack didn't want to be in the path of that swing since Les was very strong.

In addition, *The Gratiot Cats* were famous for buying junk cars and overhauling them for the fun of it. That is how Les and Earl learned the most about cars. To this day, they can fix just about anything. One day they bought a car from some folks in Ahmeek. They dragged it by hand all the way back to Gratiot—a few miles. The transmission was in need of repair, so they dumped the car over and changed the transmission themselves and turned the car back over. Billy Nowiki was perched on the fender feeding the gas, and Les was driving; the engine blew up and a piece of the engine block flew past Jack's head and nearly killed him. Because the engine block was now shot, they knew that they couldn't sell it. So they filled up the car with useless junk— metal and tires—and they dragged the car to Ripley where a guy gave them four bucks for it. They had purchased it for five, filled it with junk, and they got only four dollars for it. This time the joke was on them!

Another famous invention of the *The Gratiot Cats* was the *yukkity*. The gang would take an old car, and they would move the motor and shorten the entire chassis so that the front wheel was only six inches away from the back wheel. A flat board sat atop the motor, and the driver sat atop that with a steering wheel sticking up out of the creation. There were springs on it, so they could hit all of the dirt back roads with no problem. But one day they stopped along a state road for a few minutes. Les was on the back with a broken leg from a football game injury, and Earl was along for the ride on the yukkity, too. While stopped for a moment, Earl and Les fought there on the side of the road over who would drive the yukkity next. Les went to swing his fist at Earl as he hobbled on his one good leg, and Les missed and hit his head on a metal piece of the yukkity. Their fight ended in bloody-faced Les just about the time a state trooper appeared. He got out of his patrol car to view a yukkity by the side of the road and one bloody young man. The officer stopped and said, "What in the world is that? Where is the title and registration?" Jack said, "We don't need a registration because it's homemade: that's a yukkity!" The officer then firmly said, "Take that yukkity and never get it on this road again!" They were scared but thankful that he didn't arrest them.

Jack kept track of how many cars they bought and fixed up and he stopped counting at 120. They always paid five or six dollars for these pieces of junk that sometimes ran pretty well. On one occasion, they overhauled one motor between Mohawk and Gratiot. Another time they bought an old Ford—an old stick shift. The car went fairly fast. Les was driving the old Ford one winter day and he had the Nowiki brothers with him, each quite large themselves. Les was going around a corner into Gratiot Location—one Nowiki brother, Jigga, in the front seat along with Roy Maki and Billy Nowiki in the backseat—when he dumped the car to the left in the snow bank. Les's head got stuck between the roof and the door where the roof caved in against the driver's door. The two big brothers landed on top of him. All by himself, Les pushed the car up off of him and the two boys, besides. It very nearly killed Les. He has headaches even today as a result of that accident. One of the Nowiki boys called out, "Are you hurt, Les?" Les replied, "Of course, I'm hurt—what do you think?" Yes, they were a crazy bunch.

One afternoon, Les, Earl, and Jack decided to go for a canoe ride on Seneca Lake, each wearing his shoes, wool socks, and woolen clothing. Jack lost his balance and instead of dumping everyone, he decided to dive out. He sank like a stone with that heavy footwear. He tried swimming, but the woolen clothing weighed him down. Jack recalls, "I saw my whole life flash by and I wondered what my parents were going to say. Les and Earl were laughing and I was dying. They were paddling away and laughing, and I was yelling, 'Hey, you are going the wrong way!'" If Earl hadn't grabbed Jack by the hair and hauled him back into the canoe, he would have drowned.

If *The Gratiot Cats* wanted money, typically they would visit the dump and collect scrap metal and junk. That is basically how they made their living and bought all their cars. They would do odd jobs as well. They would all hang out at Gitche Gumee Bible Camp to help the camp directors with work around the grounds. That way they could get scholarships to go to camp. One time they had to dig a ditch by a cabin for piping of some sort. The ground turned out to be solid rock. The picking took them hours of work. They had to pick the rocks from a cottage all the way to the dining hall. But they loved the work and they also were able to attend camp. Mrs. Hart fixed pudding one time for the campers; but Les and Jack (not campers that week) ate all the pudding, so they had to shovel snow from the tabernacle roof that winter as their penalty.

Also out at camp Gitche Gumee one day, the boys discovered cherry trees by a bridge next to the camp. At midnight, they decided to raid the cherry trees that were on private property. They filled their bunks with lumpy mounds to give the appearance of sleeping campers. The next day, Pastor Hart asked them who had done this. Les, being the tenderhearted guy that he was, confessed immediately the whole ordeal. Reverend Hart made them go back and apologize to the lady that owned the cherries. She told the boys that if they had only asked, she would have given them as many as they wanted. Jack explained to her that it wouldn't have been as much fun that way—but it did teach them another lesson.

In the winter, the mines were running full blast. Gratiot Mine had a huge boiler room with five or six big furnaces providing warmth. The gang of boys would warm up and shovel coal for the miners. Then they would jump on car hoods and sail down the rock piles. They rode over one sharp rock once and split a hood right in half and nearly killed them all. It took them a half hour to haul the huge car hood up the rock pile and it took them two seconds to come flying down. Les nearly bit his tongue off sliding down the hill on one occasion when the sled went up in flight and hit a railroad tie upon landing. He sliced his tongue on his teeth from the fright of the wild ride.

When Jack was twelve years old, his mom was often drunk, so he would go over to Aunt Hazel's who adopted him eventually. Before he was adopted, the sheriff would come by and say to them that Jack's biological mom wanted her children back. So Jack was bounced back and forth from home to home. Jack's mom had a common law partner from Gratiot Location by the name of Wilfred Maki. He was part of a family that did beautiful work on building fireplaces, but they had drinking problems. Wilfred also had the epilepsy that compounded his problems. Wilfred was actually a father to Jack, and when he wasn't controlled by liquor, he was very good to Jack; but he was also the one that killed Jack's mom that evening in Gratiot Location with all the neighbors witnessing the horrific tragedy.

Another pastime of *The Gratiot Cats* was hunting. One hunting expedition took place right after Thanksgiving. There was a little bit of snow on the ground. It was late in the afternoon and they were going to Charlie Kukka's, a road that would go east from Gratiot. The guys walked down the path and it was snowing hard—so hard that when they walked in, after a little while, they couldn't see the tracks where they were before. And so in this way, Jack, Owen Isaacson, Les, and Earl made their way into the woods. Earl had an automatic 22 that didn't work very well.

Jack was the only one who had a gun that worked because he used his Uncle Chubby's guns. Owen might have had a shotgun with slugs in it, and Les had a 16-gauge shotgun. They walked to the left side of Charlie Kukka's and they went up on a ridge. They just stood on the ridge and they were watching for deer. Earl remembers, "Lo and behold, here come a big buck with the biggest rack that I have ever seen on a deer. We are standing on that mound and I said, 'Don't shoot—let him come this way.' Really, I wanted to get first shot." So the deer was pushing his nose into the snow trying to find something to eat. Then the deer took a couple of steps quickly, and Earl shot at him with the 22, but the deer needed his fill of lead from a 22 to kill him. Then as soon as Earl shot, Jack shot and Isaacson shot and Les shot and "Boom, Boom, Boom"—the deer pranced away. It was snowing hard and it was dark and they couldn't chase the deer because they would have gotten lost in the swamp. Later that winter, Les and Earl's dad found a big rack in the woods where the deer might have died and the porcupines, skunks, and coyotes ate the carcass—they ate the bones, all except the horn rack. It may have been their deer that they all thought they had missed.

There were some real characters in the gang out in Gratiot Location. People looked on them with disdain. The folks in Mohawk remember the time Jack and his buddies took a case of TNT from the mine and took a fuse and caps and put it in a powder house from the mines and exploded it, rattling windows as far away as Mohawk. But the boys didn't have anything to speak of when it came to family life. Everybody was on his own.

"Boys will be boys" as the saying goes, and these Gratiot gang members indeed filled their days with mischievous and wild behavior. But even with the fights, car accidents, brawls, murders, drunks, explosions, inventions, and expeditions, Les would glean an appreciation for deep and long-lasting friendships. As Les would say, "Life is all about relationships."

CHAPTER SIX
UTICA AVENUE

If you wed yourself to this age, you'll be a widower.

— Dr. Les Ollila

After graduating from high school in 1961, Les worked in the logging business before he went down to Detroit to help his brother Ron with a tree-topping business, but his real desire was to work later in life in the bush in the UP returning to logging and driving trucks and running large machinery. He always loved trucks and front end loaders, so he came to Detroit only to make some quick cash. He learned how to climb the ropes or use a cherry picker to climb trees. He worked with such expertise that quickly he was offered a foreman's position with a crew to work under Les's guidance. He lived with his brother Ron and worked along Utica Avenue when he first arrived.

As Ron and Les worked on Utica Avenue, Les spotted Calvary Baptist Church. Pastor Rhodes, the pastor of Calvary, recalls, "He came over that next Sunday and that was the very first Sunday that I had come as the new pastor. I had candidated in April of 1961, but this was now July. It was the first Sunday in July 1961 when Les came and he said that he liked it. And so he decided to come back the next week." The guys razzed him on the job, but Les had made up his mind that he didn't care what they said; he was going to go to church. It was within the first year there at Calvary that Les settled his salvation and began to grow even more in his Christian walk. As a young man, he had known the truth of the gospel under the Hart's ministry. But he struggled as to the certainty of his own personal relationship with Jesus Christ. Now he settled that question for sure at one service at Calvary Baptist Church. He also gave his life completely to the Lord to do whatever God asked him to do.

During this time in his life, Les sent a series of letters back to his friend, Lois Hart, and they are filled with details of his life during those tree-topping days. Here is a sampling of his early letters revealing his UP English and his experiences in Detroit:

September 5, 1961: We had a nice trip. I drove from the outside of Marquette all the way into Detroit so Stan could get some rest. We got in about 3:30; I slept in the car with my feet out the window. I feel miserable now, HA! [Many *Ha's* appear in his letters] I called you before you left but you were gone somewhere. I took Stan's car this morning and went peeling around—went to Roseville and a few other places and got some business done. I didn't see Ron yet, but I will tonight. He said that Edison is looking for a whole tree crew to go to Indiana. He wants me on it. He got me in if I want it as far as I know. I'd be gone for a whole year. I didn't say for sure yet, but it is a good deal. I start at two dollars and three cents an hour and get a raise right away. Might be lots more. I don't know where in Indiana it would be. If I go, I'm going to ask Heine, too.

I'd have to pray about it first because if it was a bad move, I would be stuck there for a year. It's a good steady job; I could save a lot in that time. I'll know more about it after tonight. It's really hot here now. I was sweating bullets when I was driving. But I'm in the office. I'm a big wheel now. I'm writing this letter behind Stan's desk in his office air-conditioned and all. It makes me look important to the passers by—HA!

November 27, 1961: Well, it didn't take me long to get a job. I got one the day that I got down here. I can thank the Lord for that. Ron took me to the office with him and said that I wanted a job. They put me on crew before I filled my application blank even. Even Ron didn't expect to get me in that quick. I'm starting at three dollars an hour. They put me on as first year climber. I'll be staying at Ron's. I'll have to come home and get my car and come right back—that miserable drive again.

December 1961: I'm bowling now on Heath Tree's Company team. We went last Thursday. There are twenty-eight alleys where we go. Ronnie is the captain and he wanted me to bowl and so I went for the laughs.

January 2, 1962: [He asks about Lois's trip to Chicago when she went as a senior.] I'll bet you had a lot of fun milling around in them stores, eh?, I thought that you would send a card, but I guess that you were too busy. I finally got rid of that miserable Ford. I bought a new Chevy Bel Air. It's real nice. It's fire engine red; inside is all red, too just like Ronnie's. You saw his—it's a hard top like my Ford was, white walls, radio; it has everything on it. I got it Saturday and drove it right out of the showroom. I was having a lot of trouble with that Ford. I would have had to spend a lot of money on it, so I decided to get a different one. I thought about buying a used car but I thought twice about it; I figured that I would get someone else's troubles, so I felt that I was best off buying a new one. I needed a dependable car real bad anyway. You'll have fun driving that one—nice piece of machinery.

January 15, 1962: I got a part in a young people's program last Sunday. We're putting on a skit on juvenile delinquency in the community. I met the youth director and I said that I'd like to take part in the group. He asked me first, and I told him I would. I've been asked to join the choir but it was just talk. [The church was sincere, but this was Les's self-defacing way.] They rehearse on Wednesday after prayer meeting. They said they'd like to work me into the tenor section. There's about 320-350 in Sunday School. The youth group isn't too big and it needs prayer. I'd like to be some help in some way with the Lord's help. Our Sunday School lessons are interesting. We're studying a regular book on the O.T. survey. It's like a regular course. The book costs $1.25. I may learn something from it. One of the church's missionaries spoke yesterday Sunday morning—really interesting. He showed slides. He's from the Congo; that's where all that warring is going on right now. You read about it quite often in the papers. He had some interesting stories to tell. My ma wrote and said that Russell Heikkila would be at the church soon, eh, so I guess that is what she said. She said that she and dad were going if I am right about this. Give them a call and invite them out, ok?

January 1962: We had a good trip; it seemed so short, it seemed like we went for a ride to Houghton or something. Owen didn't find a job yet but I guess he's still looking. When he's eighteen, I am almost positive that he can get in where I'm working. The supervisor asked me if I had any more brothers. He said that he'd hire them all. Owen's no relative, but we can put in a good word for him.

February 1, 1962: I still got my cold; it's kind of hard to shake when you have to work outside in the cold every day. I've been eating pills and drinking all kinds of dopes. It's kind of breezy way up in some of them trees. There's no protection at all. Ron and I did a private job Saturday. A big poplar tree. I went up in it to do the stripping. It was way in the air and leaning over a house. I thought I was going to kick the bucket up there. I was coughing so much. It really felt good to get into the sauna. We went two nights in a row. There are a couple of saunas down here that I know of. I'm thinking about Bible school, but I doubt that I'll be able to go to school next year but you have a good idea. After next year, I'll have my car paid for and should have a good amount in the bank. If the Lord leads me, well then I'll go and won't have to worry about the money. I shouldn't worry about it anyway. I could still do tree work on weekends and make good money. So you think that you'll surprise me one of these nights, eh, HA! When I come home, I'm half sleeping and my eyes are half shut. I'd probably walk right past you if you were on the couch and go straight to bed. That would be funny if it actually happened, eh. I can just imagine you sitting there watching me go by. I wish you would come down sometime though. I would like to know when your folks are coming down. Send me the dates; I'd like to see them. I may get up there sometime too just for a spin. I lost about 5 pounds myself. I'm eating more now than I ever did, too. That climbing is hard work. Sometimes I guess that's what keeps my bony frame trim. My car's been running fine. It sure feels good to have something reliable; it's a little better than the thumb [he drew a thumb] used to be, HA. Remember, I used to head for the junction feeling miserable. I used to always say I'd never let Earl use my car if I got one, but I guess I'd let him have it.

March 1962: I worked last Saturday, me and another guy from the crew. We trimmed some big maples. Made $36.50 each in seven hours. It was quite a lot of extra work there, too.

April 62: I talked to Earl last night he said that he might be coming down. It will be good for some heavy-duty laughs. Ron called home to see how dad was doing so we were able to talk to everyone. So your dad will be getting that new car, eh? That sure will be nice after all the heartache, woe, and strife than that *pushalla* [old faithful station wagon] he had.

June 1962 [A comment on the beaches down in Detroit]: It's been raining down here quite a bit lately. At least it's not as warm as usual. It's useless to try to get on some of these beaches around here. You'd feel just as rotten when you leave as when you got there anyhow.

July 8, 1962: Friday night I went to a singspiration on the Detroit River. It was a lot of fun. There were kids from all over. Our group went down on the bus. I was voted Vice President of the young people's group. I was kind of surprised to hear that. It will keep me more on my toes I guess. I'm sending some money to send someone to camp. It sure can bless your life. A person never realizes until he gets outside into the world how important Christian backing means. It probably seems dumb for me to be writing again so soon, but I had to. I hope you don't want to shoot me. I forgot all about your birthday; I was just thinking today that your birthday is going to be soon and then I thought, holy smokes, your birthday is already past. I hope you will forgive me.

August of 62: We got rained out today, so I had an easy day, just sat around. Ron and I are doing quite a bit of private work now. We made $75.00 each last Saturday. So I made $195.00 last week. It would be nice if we got those jobs every weekend. We are working on small jobs here and there. At least it's something. I'm getting a pretty good bankroll. If the radio broadcast [Christian radio station by Gitche Gumee camp] is still going, I'd still like to help in that if I could. I'm going to have to find out who to write to about changing membership.

In the meantime, Lois Hart was very interested in another young man. But God had this all planned—a lovely young woman named Charlene came into Les's life. Charlene was a small child when her mom died; and as her dad worked, she lived with various relatives and moved from place to place. In her teen years, she went to live with Pastor Bob and Marcella Rhodes. She lived with them during their ministry in Sedalia, Missouri. When the Rhodes took the pastorate in Roseville, Michigan, it was natural for Charlene to go up north with the Rhodes and their family. Charlene had gone to school in South Carolina; in the summer, she would visit her Aunt who lived in Detroit. On one particular visit, she decided to stay with Rhodes instead of her aunt in the summer of 1962.

One afternoon in 1962 while Les was working on the tree-topping, he got to do some soul-searching. He was struck with the thought, "An ape could do this; I want to do something with my life that will glorify God." So down he came from the tree and told his buddies that he was done. He surrendered his life at church the following Sunday to be a preacher. That same Sunday, he met a lovely young woman, Charlene. Les still worked another year at the tree-topping but wrestled all the while with his decision.

Les was more shy about Charlene than his commitment to God, so the Rhodes had to help things along. Les was getting ready to go up north one Saturday morning to help Charlie Hill fix his car. Pastor Rhodes recalls, "I called Les and I said that we want to get Charlene over here and we've got something going on and would you pick Charlene up and bring her over?" So the Rhodes' matchmaking really paid off. They could tell that he wouldn't take the initiative, and they thought that Les and Char were interested in each other, so it was the perfect opportunity. He was walking out the door to head up north and the phone rang just then. Les's response was "Oh yes, I'll be glad to go get her." He brought her over and asked her out for their first date. At Christmas, 1962, when she was back in Roseville from Bob Jones University, Les asked her to marry him.

Lois Hart recalls those events: "I didn't get another letter from him from August which is the time he met Char until February of 1963 when I heard that he was engaged and wrote him to congratulate him and he wrote back telling me about Char. At the time, I was interested in another guy that I was writing to and I was really happy to hear that Les was getting married and I felt happy for him." That letter in '63 arrived putting closure to Lois and Les's relationship while maintaining their friendship. Les wrote:

February of 1963: I was surprised to receive your letter, but it was good to hear from you. It seems like a long time since we've seen or heard from each other. Yes, I am an engaged man and happily so. I got engaged at Christmas. Earl knew when he was home, but he didn't say anything. I suppose it was a surprise to a lot of people but that always seems to be the case. She is a wonderful Christian girl, a little older than I am, eight months. I really love her; the Lord just worked things out perfectly. We prayed very definitely for the Lord's will in the matter. I met her at church the week after I came back from up North in September. It seemed just that we were attracted to each other. There are a few things that happened that make us more sure of the Lord's leading and it just makes us praise the Lord. She is a hillbilly from Sedalia, Missouri, from ya'all land. The pastor of our church is from there and she was staying with them for a couple of weeks before she went back to school. That's how I happened to meet her. The week after I came from up home, she was at church for the first time. I was introduced to her and I thought that she was a pretty nice girl, but I didn't have any intentions of doing anything about it, but a few things went on and it seemed that we were for each other. It takes awhile to explain. The Lord sure has definite ways of working. We didn't have a lot of time to go out because she had to go back to school. Before she left, we had a prayer asking the Lord's leading in our lives. He worked everything out perfectly. She's a sophomore at

Bob Jones University in South Carolina, and she works in Detroit in the summer though she's from Missouri. The pastor from our church had a church in Sedalia before he came here. That's where Charlene went, so when she was here, she stayed with them. They are a wonderful couple just like your mom and dad—a little younger. They have two girls that remind me of Ginger and Patty. I don't know if I should have told you all of this or not, but I thought that you would be curious to hear what kind of a girl I got tangled up with, HA! The Lord has blessed in my life in the past five or six months. I dedicated my life for Him to use me in any way He wants to use me. I thank God he has given me the strength to live for Him. It sure is a blessing to do service for the Lord. I'll just say that I'm the same old me and getting along pretty good. Still working steady and all—sorta cold once in awhile, though—hard on monkeys. I'm planning to go to Bob Jones this fall so I'll probably be hitting the books again. At least I'm ready to go and know that it is the Lord's will. When I got out of high school, college did not appeal to me in the least. But now I feel that the Lord can use me somewhere in His service. I want to wish you all the happiness in life so that is straightened out I guess. I guess the both of us wondered about each other which is natural so I hope that this letter will clear things up. May God bless you and be near to you in your future.

In the summer of 1963, after Char had finished her sophomore year of college, Les still fought the idea of college for himself. Pastor Rhodes encouraged him that if he really felt called to be a preacher that he needed some training. Charlene had a promise box with verses from the Scriptures for each day. One day Charlene read Jeremiah 33:3 to Les: "Call unto me and I will answer thee and show thee great and mighty things which thou knowest not." That was his answer. He would yield to the Lord even though book learning was the last thing he wanted to go back to. Charlene completed her junior year at Bob Jones University and Les entered the dorms for his first year. After Les's first year, they were then married in June of 1964. They lived in Essex Court behind Quality Inn in Greenville, South Carolina. Charlene dropped out of college to help Les through his next three years.

Utica Avenue had led to far more dreams than Les had ever anticipated. His desire to hide in the woods behind a pay loader had been swept aside because the passion of his heart now became a desire to be in the ministry. The young lad who helped drunk neighbors and who went to the big city to cut tops of trees, now faced an adventure of faith that would rival all of his past experiences.

Les as a youngster

Working at Gitche Gumee

Les's first exposure to the gospel, Evangelist Phil Ward

Earl Ollila, Jimmy Hill and Les

Jack Spreitzer and Earl Ollila, Les sleeping

The Hart Hotel

Les's high school graduation

Gratiot Location, Ollila home

Gratiot Location home in 2003

Les's red Bel Air

Les and Charlene with Gratiot neighbors

Inside Gratiot home 2003

Les visits birthplace

Les's graduation from Bob Jones University

Pastor Charles and Joyce Hart

Les with Rod Bell and Marty Von

Children attend Calvary Baptist Church in Roseville, MI for Bibletime because of Les's leadership in outreach

Les, Charlene, Lisa, and Tami in Roseville Ministry

Les's winning ways

Les and Charlene at high school banquet

Roseville youth sponsors

Les receives honorary doctorate; Bob Jones Jr. and Bob Jones III

Les, Charlene, Lisa, Tami, and Steven after arriving at Northland

Honored guests at Dr. Ollila's inauguration as president of Northland Baptist Bible College

Dr. Monroe Parker and Bob Jones Jr. with Les at his inauguration

Early days of Northland, Les preaching

Les's first office at Northland

Dr. R.V. Clearwaters with Les

One of Les's favorite hobbies

Les demonstrates tree-topping at Lumberjack Days

Partners in mischief, Les and Marty Von

Les with high school English teacher Dave Coltman

Heart Conference speakers

Einard and Sophie Ollila, Les's parents

Einard, Sophie, and children

Les, Charlene, and family

Les, Charlene, Lisa, Tami, and Steven

Dr. and Mrs. Ollila

Charlene

Les

Honorary hockey team member

Daily chapel at Northland Baptist Bible College

Chancellor, Dr. Les Ollila with President, Dr. Matt Olson

Chancellor Ollila

Chapter Seven
The Foreman

Always be a learner.

— Dr. Les Ollila

No, book learning was not the favored focus for Les to direct his efforts, but in 1963, Les entered the dormitories of Bob Jones University, a well-known Christian university. He had finally overcome his lisp and his stammering. A county therapist during his high school years helped him learn how to speak. Les had to practice placing his tongue onto the roof of his mouth rather than over his front teeth. It took much practice and discipline. Then his college speech teachers at Bob Jones guided his recovery from this problem, too. This Upper Peninsula "hick" entered a fine religious southern school with all of its "proper" ways. His suitcase contained the one sport coat that he owned. This meant that Les would be met with some interesting trials immediately.

For instance, Les and his roommates that first year got wind of the fact that some guys down the hall were making fun of the clothes that a student, named Les Ollila, would wear. So Les marched down the hall one day to confront this fellow student. He lifted up the student completely off the floor, turned him upside down, and while the guilty party hung there by his feet, Les informed him that he was never to make fun of his clothing again. That student had sorely underestimated the strength of this logger from the woods of upper Michigan. Les's "counseling methods" mellowed a bit after those initially bumpy days of adjusting to a dormitory filled with young men, who for the most part, knew only loving Christian homes and southern propriety and finery.

It took Les a while to adjust to the "formal" studies, but he soaked in his theology classes because his heart was to know God's Word and to be able to share its truths with others in a deep, rich way. However, parts of the requirements for his first year were to take English classes. He remembers being overwhelmed with the studies of Shakespeare. "What in the world was this author trying to say?" To cope with this class work, he nicknamed Shakespeare, "Billy Wiggledagger." He still refers to Shakespeare as Billy Wiggledagger even when he quotes something from him today. His humor came out once again to add the needed laughs to those early college days.

Charlene was faithfully working as a secretary while Les went through his schooling there at Bob Jones. After their marriage in 1964, when he finished his freshmen year and she completed her junior year, she patiently waited to complete her education until after he had completed his. Les's talents quickly became known in the city, and he began to work on crews of large machinery for construction. He worked himself up to a foreman position, and he managed to lead a crew of guys with the job of building the new facilities around the university.

For example, in 1965, Fred Davis, an employee of Bob Jones University, and Les were co-workers to see the completion of the Dining Commons for the campus of the university. They had to replace what was the Winn Dixie grocery store with a dining facility that could feed thousands in one sitting. Les was put in charge of the building crew because the contractors employed him. They had previously employed another foreman that had gotten too ill to be able to do the work, so the construction superintendent suggested that Les take the position as a replacement. The contractors saw immediately how much of a serious-minded, purpose-driven boss they had hired. Les's co-worker Fred was overseer of the general project for the university. The crew that worked under Les consisted of some students, but men from the surrounding city were employees as well.

This began another of Les's friendships. His goal to build people had permeated all of his endeavors over the years. Fred was so impressed with the character of this young man who directed an entire crew to build a very large dining facility in the space of six months. In 1965, it was almost unheard of to build such a building in that amount of time. But Les was a no-nonsense boss. Whenever he walked in the door in the morning, the crew jumped up off their seats and they would declare, "We're just on break," or "We just stopped to check on some things." Les had respect for his workers and they respected him in turn. He was a driver and pusher of the crew, a good worker, and an example himself, but no one could say that he was not always congenial through it all.

Fred has a tremendous respect for Les to this day. He characterizes him in this way: "Les is my good friend—my lifelong friend. He is a spiritual man, a godly man, and he had great respect from those crewmen. He was a good witness for the Lord to them and he was the perfect guy for the job." Not only did they work on the Dining Commons together, but also Les was the foreman for other crews to develop the campus further. Fred says of Les's future position, "Les was the right man for the job as president [1984–2002] at Northland Baptist Bible College. He is smart and energetic. I respect him highly." There is nothing like comradery that is built as men work together with mutual drive and energy to see difficult tasks accomplished. That was true of Fred and Les.

One evening Fred recalls that he was on the job alone late at night. He noticed a suspicious vehicle that drove into the parking lot near the Dining Commons on the campus. It was rather scary, and he also noticed that there were two thug-like figures in the car. He never would have been any match for these guys. He was quite leery of their intentions, and he kept a very good eye on them. Their shadows were those of bulky men filling the seats of the sedan. The streetlight passing through the back windows accentuated their shadows. Fred could not avoid a confrontation, so he watched the men approach. Fred's sigh was audible when he found out that they were looking for Les and they turned out to be Les's brother Heine and one of Heine's friends. Whew! He was glad that he was in one piece that night after wondering about these mysterious mountain men.

While Charlene was busy as a secretary to pay Les's bills for college, and while Les was studying during the wee hours of the mornings to get through school, and while they were struggling to make the payments for all of their other living expenses, they also poured themselves into ministry on the weekends. Their love for the "down and outers" of society would walk them right into a hotbed of the drunk and disorderly. The next few years were yet another test of their faith as they launched out into local church work. Les and Charlene never sat still. Life was never about, "What can we do to fulfill our dreams in this world?" Life was about, "What can we do to make a difference in the lives of others?" What an example they were as a young couple!

So the youngster from Gratiot Location with the lisping speech and the shy demeanor commanded his studies and led work crews for local contractors. The leadership responsibilities piled on his shoulders, and he was becoming a leader to train future leaders.

Chapter Eight
Bootleg Corner

You will always be relevant if you speak eternal truth.

— Dr. Les Ollila

In the fall of 1960, Dr. Rod Bell, graduate of Bob Jones University was asked to start a little mission church in a section of Greenville, South Carolina. A friend named Dr. Sightler took Dr. Bell to "a dirty, dingy corner [...] run down, with rotten buildings. We pulled up in front of an old service station garage and parked." He said, "This is where we want to start it. Here's an available building" (Bell, *Mantle* 80). Dr. Sightler helped them pay the first month's rent and then Dr. Bell was on his own. "Ostracized by the progressive neighboring villages, some residents turned to bootlegging, and none were more prominent than Bootleg Corner's leading citizen, Mrs. Tine Center, known to all as 'Fat Ma.' She and her daughter, Hazel, became distributors for moonshine peddlers out of the mountains of western North Carolina" ("History" 1). The Bells cleaned up the building and began to go to the neighborhood and share the Gospel with folk and invited them to come out to services. Rod Bell writes in his autobiography:

> *Little did we know, however, that we were facing unseen opposition. This area [of Greenville] was used as a depot for a syndicate that brought bootleg*

liquor out of the North Carolina mountains. It was an ideal distribution point because, although it was in Greenville County, it was outside both the Greenville and the City View city limits. The locals called it "Red Egypt" because of the sin and vice. The only law enforcement authority was the County Sheriff's Department, but they usually looked the other way when it came to this neighborhood. (Bell, Mantle 80)

In 1965, Dr. Les Ollila was one of the deacons at the church that partnered in the ministry to see the church make a go of it. Since Les grew up around people that were controlled by the drink, he did whatever it took to be a support in the ministry at Bootleg Corner. In addition, Dr. Bell writes, "Les was our handyman—a servant. Whatever needed to be done, he did it—cleaning, fixing, cutting trees, teaching, and preaching" (Bell, Email).

They fought against all odds in that particular ministry. They lived through death threats, fear of reprisal, and fist fights. Dr. Bell could depend on Les to support him. He shared in an Email interview that "whatever needed to be done, Les did it. His loyalty and servant's heart are 'sterling' qualities. Les stood with me and helped me pastor the church. When we were under fire from the bootleggers and the community which did not want our church there, and when there was rebellion among some of the people, I could count on Les to watch my back" (Bell, Email). One man named Bill Hughes had told Dr. Bell that the next time anyone came to his door and preached to him that Bill would shoot him. Les was one of the guys that went to Bill's door again. Bill let the preacher boys in and then pulled out his shotgun and told them that now he would do the "preachin.'" Dr. Bell and Les and others kept encouraging Bill to give his life to Christ. Bill said, "I have served the devil for fifty-some years. He has wrecked my home; he's wrecked my body, he's ruined my health; he's robbed food out of my children's mouths; he's damned my soul. I have nothing to show for fifty-some years but heartache and trouble and disappointment. The devil has stripped me of my manhood" (Bell, *Mantle* 84). Dr. Bell later had the joy of pointing that man to Christ. He accepted Christ as his Savior and found out what God could now do with a life dedicated to serving Him.

The church sensed a need to have a decent building because the congregation had grown to 250 members. During one Friday night prayer meeting, anticipating still future growth in the ministry, the men took off their shoes and marched around the kudzu-filled dumping ground along Cedar Lane Road and claimed it for the Lord. Nearly 20 years later (1985), without any knowledge of that marching prayer meeting, the church would purchase that property and in 1991 would construct its present auditorium on the piece of property claimed by these men so many years before ("History" 2). The church is presently named Mount Calvary Baptist Church.

However, here is where Les really comes in. Rod Bell left to plant a church in Virginia. The strife in the summer of 1967 grew in the little South Carolina church to the point that the church attendance dropped from 250 to 17 within a matter of weeks. Les and Charlene had been back in Roseville, Michigan, to be ordained; and when they returned to Bootleg Corner, the church had dwindled. Rod Bell writes of Les, "Had it not been for Les during my resignation and his interim pastoring, the church would have closed" (Bell, Email). Although Les had a full-time job at the time, he accepted a position of interim pastor in 1967 and built the church back up to over one hundred. God used Les to refresh the church with new Christians, and he began the rebuilding process. Les and Charlene were then asked to go back to Roseville, Michigan, where he was ordained to take the youth pastorate.

Rod Bell sums it all up this way: "I thank God for the little spot of ground where Les, Charlene, Lenore and I learned to pray" (Bell, Email). Being in the "people-business" was harder than any task Les had faced. When he came to the end of himself, his resources, and his ingenuity, God was showing Les and Charlene to place their faith fully in Him and His guidance.

Chapter Nine
Uncle Les in Roseville

Pinpoint your passion.

— Dr. Les Ollila

On the heels of the interim pastorate in Bootleg Corner in 1968, Pastor Rhodes needed a secretary desperately and he knew that Charlene was an excellent one. "I've never seen anyone type as fast as she does and take shorthand. I *mean* she *is* an excellent secretary. And so I told the deacons that I would like to go down [to South Carolina] and interview Charlene for my secretary." Les teases Pastor Rhodes to this day because Charlene did accept the position and they made Les the youth pastor. So they got Charlene and Les in one package. What they did not know was the next few years, 1968 through 1975, were to be the years that Les Ollila turned the world of Roseville upside down for Christ.

This would have been his first ministry as a youth pastor. His passion was to love young people, bring the parents on board, and train sponsors to carry on the ministry themselves. He was young, but his wisdom exceeded his years. He met with some resistance in his new ministry like any other minister would. One night on a bus after a youth program they had attended where the music was "Christian rock" and the program void of solid truth for teens, Les stood on the bus and said, "I'm taking my stand here and now; I don't care if any of you stand with me or not; we'll never come back to a program like this because the music was horrible and the program terrible and we're not gonna do it, and we are taking a position. If you don't agree with me, take a hike!" Amazingly enough, all the young people gravitated to his genuine tough love. Nobody deserted him, so he was free to run the program of discipleship and leadership training that he envisioned. He was a visionary from the start—he was the forerunner of the family seminar before there were formal family seminar speakers. He was a "nouthetic" counselor before the term was coined. Nouthetic counseling gets to the heart of a problem and applies Biblical answers. It stresses the sufficiency of the Word of God to meet the daily needs in the lives of believers. The Bible takes precedence over modern psychology. Now a National Association for Nouthetic Counselors exists for Biblical counselors all over the country. But Les applied these principles as a young youth pastor. The young people saw an example of someone completely transparent, and they were drawn to him. His method of casual discipleship meant that if he took a tree-topping job, he never went alone. He would call one of the young men that he felt had potential as a leader and would take him on a tree-topping job to talk with him and ask questions that would cause that young person to think. If he planned to go to McDonalds for coffee, he would invite a teen to go along. If he were going to the hardware store, he took someone along.

Notably, his "napkin theology" began during these days. He couldn't speak without writing something down. He would pull out several napkins from the dispenser and sketch something practical for these young people to understand. If they faced a crisis, he would encourage them to take the fruit of the Spirit listed in the book of Galatians and ask God which fruit needed to be perfected in a person's life through a particular trial. Was it patience, peace, joy, longsuffering, meekness? Or he would take the great love chapter in the Bible, I Corinthians 13, and he would explain that they needed to ask God to incorporate all the aspects of love into their lives. "Love is kind, patient, seeks not its own, is not easily provoked." All the answers are there for the Christian to grow and become a real example instead of a hypocrite.

The magnet in Les's ministry was that he did not have a proud bone in his body. Pastor Rhodes related these memories:

> *Les is the most humble man I will ever know. Many times during the church service, we would have a visiting speaker come in and he would give an invitation and Les would be the first one down the aisle. I've never seen an assistant pastor or youth pastor like him—he was so humble. So meek and mild yet he could be fired up with those young people. He laid down the law; he was a good blend of tough and tender.*

When young people knew that Les was real and that he really loved them, they responded with complete pliability. Les had that magnetic, genuine gift.

Another aspect of being the second man is the danger that you will take away the spotlight from the pastor's ministry, but Les was the perfect "second man." Les and Pastor Rhodes got together one day in the beginning of the ministry at Roseville, and they agreed to make each other successful—the key to being a team player. So many senior pastors are destroyed because the assistant pastor diverts loyalty his way, or the competition becomes carnal (in the flesh and not directed Godward) and self-centered. Sometimes the senior pastor does not support the ministry of the assistant and thus undermines the credibility of the second man. The second man is then dead in the water. However, Les and Pastor Rhodes kept mutual loyalty throughout Les's entire ministry at Roseville. Pastor Rhodes sat down with paper and pen and figured out one day that about 135 to 150 young people came out of that Roseville ministry and went on to be missionaries, pastors, or full-time Christian workers during the ministry of his church. He did say, moreover, that almost all of them came from that time period when Les was their youth pastor.

Pastor Rhodes was never jealous for his pulpit. He let Les preach often because he believed that if someone is called to be a preacher, he should practice preaching. Pastor Rhodes was a wonderful facilitator for Les to blossom as he discovered his talents and calling in the ministry. "Les always had such a knack of saying things just exactly the right way. I've never heard anyone speak quite like him. He can pinpoint. He is saying what you are thinking. He can say offensive things in such a way that you'd love him for it. Other people can say it—I can say nice things and people get offended. That is the difference between Les and me." They really made an effective duo.

Pastor and Les would go calling together, too, to get needy kids to come on buses to Sunday School. They would go up and down the street and meet at the other end. Les would report that he had large numbers of people that would promise to come and Pastor struggled to get any. Pastor Rhodes remembers, "He'd get handfuls of candidates [for the bus ministry] to pick up and I'd get none. We could switch sides and it didn't matter." It was his down-to-earth, what-you-see-is-what-you-get ability to win the hearts of strangers.

Les, however, would be the first to say that he was not the detail person. One time, Les sent Pastor Rhodes out on a call to a lady in town. Specifics were not his forte. He gave pastor the address and said that the lady's name was Mrs. Canada. So pastor left and said that he would try to stop and meet her and visit with her to see if he could be of any help. He parked his car in a community near Roseville, and he walked up to the door and rang the bell. A lady came to the door and the pastor said, "Are you Mrs. Canada?"

She looked at him funny and said, "No, I'm Mrs. London." Maybe Les was thinking London, Ontario, Canada. She actually was the correct lady that Les wanted Pastor to visit, but Pastor Rhodes is still trying to figure that one out.

"Life is funny if you look at it the right way" is the philosophy that Les took with him through his ministry. When he was tired and coming home from some meetings or visiting, he said that he knew he was truly wiped out because he saw elephants on skateboards and turkeys with tin hats. He knew it was time to pull over and catch a nap when that happened.

Les and Pastor Rhodes both learned in their counseling ministries to let themselves laugh to keep perspective. There was one lady in town that would call them both and they knew that she was "half a load short," or whatever expression one wants to use. She would call and read Pastor Rhodes and Les the riot act. One time Pastor Rhodes was in Les's office and the phone was lying down and someone was talking on the phone. Les was working away doing something else and Pastor noticed that he would pick the receiver up and say, "Uh, huh," and then he would put it back down and he would keep working. It was that particular lady. She would call and never say "Hello." She would say, "Why can't the Indians vote in this country?" or "Father so and so at Sacred Heart has gotten together with you and now the postmaster is reading my mail." All kinds came their way, and so they were able to laugh at themselves and their circumstances.

During his counseling days, Les decided from observation that most people just wanted to hear themselves talk instead of wanting to change some habit in their lives. This is where "nouthetic" counseling started before there was the National Association of Nouthetic Counselors. He made up his own "prescription" pad. Jerry Hairgrove, a dear friend of the Ollilas who worked with Les in Roseville relates, "I do remember. He started running into a lot of people that did not really want to change. He developed a Bible prescription pad. One of the first questions that he would ask is, 'Do you want to change and are you willing to obey God?' He had a little pad of paper like the doctor's. He designed one." It was then the person's responsibility to go and do what the first step was and if he returned with the first responsibility completed, then Les as the counselor knew that this person was really interested in changing and not just spouting off to someone. Along with prescriptions, he developed the daily dozen verbal vitamins. For example, "K" for kindness would be a daily vitamin. He was fun, innovative, creative, pointed, and very influential in the lives of so many that he counseled. His wisdom was evident beyond his true number of years. One youth sponsor helping Les observed, "Les lived in poverty by today's standards. From his background with speech problems and his desire to be a logger or drive semi, it just depicts what God can do with someone who is willing, regardless of talent."

What made his youth ministry unique? He was an ordinary guy from a rough background that was totally sold on a cause with passion, and he let God lead him to develop a well-balanced youth program that involved the entire church ministry led by the right people. Dave and Joyce Weirich took a job with Ford in Detroit and moved to the area and joined Calvary Baptist Church in Roseville. They were young and eager to help in the church ministry. They were recruited by Les to be some of his youth sponsors. Les had other dynamic dedicated couples that joined his efforts. For eleven years, Dave and Joyce poured their lives into young people there at Calvary Baptist Church of Roseville. Barb Corey, a fellow member of the church said, "Les presented truths of the Scriptures and made them come alive for you. Young people picked up on that." His youth ministry was wide-ranging and comprehensive.

One aid was the three-ring binders that were filled with notes and helps for the young people, sponsors, and parents. It was a virtual practical theology manual. Les ran two programs, one for the junior high and one for the senior high because of maturity levels physically, emotionally, and spiritually. He split these into groups and then the teens were split within those groups and sponsors had oversight for those smaller groups. Sunday night before the evening church service, they had the youth meetings.

Sessions usually lasted one hour; they also had meetings on Wednesday nights. Les would write lessons for the week and the teen groups would come at 5 o'clock on Sunday night for teen choir. During that time, Les would train parents. Then at 6 pm, the young people would present their lessons in skit form or drama. Then regular church services were at 7 pm. The whole day was one of training and Christian fellowship.

Also, his youth activities were never the run-of-the-mill activities. There were the senior banquets for the high school graduates and the meals were served on location in everything from real 747's to cruise ships. Nothing was too great to go for. Joyce Weirich remembers those moments of preparation: "We worked a lot for those senior banquets. I remember sponsor ladies getting together and we would make programs that were elaborate—No computers! We made our own centerpieces, peanut cups, the whole shebang." One year the group went to Meadowbrook Hall, a lovely mansion on the Oakland University Campus. Dave Weirich remembers clearly: "I did a lot of planning for many of these banquets. When we got to the mansion, they said they were sorry and they overbooked. 'If you don't mind,' they went on, 'we'll put you in the boardroom library on a velvet carpet.' It was beautiful—like a king's palace." The group filed into this palatial banquet hall and they were treated royally as well. There was a pipe organ. To get its sound throughout the building, it went into underground tunnels and then through hollows in the walls so one could hear the organ through this huge mansion. The banquet facilities were so impressed with the good behavior of the group that the man in charge came and asked if anyone played the organ. Sharon Rhodes, pastor's daughter, approached this huge pipe organ and started playing. Dave also relates, "Les was the spark plug for social things; he threw out the ideas and we ran with them." Sponsors and teens never forget those memorable events.

Les also rigged crazy scavenger hunts. The Polaroid hunts were wild as the young people went out in their groups and had to return with pictures of them in unusual situations: in a phone booth with a nun, or with a police officer in jail, or anything wild. They all loved it. What fun it was! One night poor Dave Weirich was a driver for one scavenger hunt. The young people had to gather pizza ingredients on this trip and the first team to put together an edible pizza and bake it would win. Dave shared, "On one occasion, I had just gotten a new car, and these kids were mixing a pizza in the back seat of my new car." The other young people were up in the front seat mixing dough. The one kid says, "Turn on the heat full blast." It was summer time, by the way. Anyhow, they held the dough under the blasting heater and sure enough, the dough was rising as they were speeding their way back to church. The group with Dave Weirich could hardly breath in the car with the heat on full blast. They ended up putting bologna on the pizza and it actually tasted quite delicious.

From Les's days as the youth pastor, every teen remembers the Halloween parties in the woods. All year long the young people prepared for this big event. They would choose someone's yard that had dark, dense forest, or they would get permission to work on an abandoned house. One year there was a family who had lots of trees and trails, and they said that the youth could work there. They worked feverishly with Neal Cushman as one of the teens that led the pack. They built a trail through the woods belonging to one of the church members from New Baltimore. It was a lovely spot with a nice forest and seclusion. They dug a tunnel that one had to walk down into and there was an electric chair; and teens would get shocked and then climb up a ladder, and then they would walk down this trail and these monsters and guys in camouflage would jump out. Some of them would be rigged on trolleys and come flying out of the trees. They had dry ice on a pond along the path, and they even had a monster come up out of the pond. One guy, Craig Sikkelee, had to be in a cage and they pasted hair to his chest as if he were a wild man beating on the cage.

One hard worker preparing for these events, Neal Cushman, remembers, "We built a 15-foot spider out of paper mache' one time; and we got hair from the barbershops of all of Detroit, all of this black hair, and we glued it on and we put up this spider in a gap over people's heads." One thing that happened that was not so good was that they built a grave and they had Earl Ollila lying in the graveyard like a corpse. Some of the kids got the great idea of throwing rocks. Earl came up out of the grave and tackled those guys. They didn't try that again—that's for sure. Les allowed the kids the freedom to create and have fun. He was right in the middle of them like another teenager. He was just as excited as they were.

Les pulled a fast one on the teens one night after one of those Halloween scary nights. He faked the bus's stalling and he had planted several sponsors off the road. He had the young people get out and help him push the bus. These men came out of the ditches and from behind trees and out of the woods and scared those kids to death. The teens were all ripe for this surprise after the evening that they had just experienced.

His own young people that eventually became sponsors characterize him as somebody who was universally liked. Neal and Pam Cushman characterize him this way: "He was the guy that wasn't afraid to play football and baseball and do things and make home visits and spend time with you." Neal and Pam also remember how busy the ministry was in the summers, but Les took a different approach than he did during the school year. The young people would take special summer trips with a "Salt" emphasis: "Souls Are Lost Today" or "Save All Lost Teens" as the motto. "We would gather at church on Saturday and we would spend a time in challenge studying the Bible, time of prayer, and we would go out visiting teens together," Neal fondly remembers.

It is what Les shows to people in his life that endears him to so many especially from the Roseville days. When Neal Cushman's stepfather died, Neal and his wife, Pam, had been away from the ministry in Roseville for sometime and were missionaries in Nova Scotia, Canada. However, the funeral for Neal's stepfather was in Roseville. Les was across the country somewhere, but guess who showed up at the door of the church where the funeral was? Les Ollila. He was like that. He always wanted to fill the need in someone's life. His insight endeared him to hundreds of teens and their families for a lifetime.

Earl became Les's right hand man on the youth trips. Earl was living in Roseville by this time and he made a terrific bus driver/handyman. One time they had a problem with the clutch on the old Greyhound church bus. If someone could drive a bus, Les always said that he could be a good youth pastor. At least he could drive the kids someplace where they would be influenced by camp or some other speakers. Bus troubles were common, but at those times, Earl and Les were thankful for their mechanical expertise from the Upper Peninsula days. Anyway, the clutch went out in the middle of Philadelphia somewhere. Earl was on his hands and knees working the clutch, Tim Zimmerman was lifting the gas pedal, and Les was driving. So Les would yell, "OK clutch!" And so Earl would have to push the clutch with his hand because the foot pedal wouldn't work. And so the three of them had to drive the bus in this fashion until they could stop long enough to get it fixed. This was sometimes a typical scenario—bus problems!

Jerry and Cheryl Hairgrove remember the Roseville days, but Jerry especially remembers the "flashbacks." Les would take pictures of everything all throughout the year and then on senior banquets he would show slides. Jerry said, "The sponsors and the teens saw it as a unifying connection. That was the glue—his caring and loving the teens so much. And investing his life." After college, Jerry asked Les if he could come to Roseville and just observe Les in action with the young people. Jerry aspired to be a youth pastor someday and there was no one else he would rather follow around to learn from. Les said, sure. So Jerry watched Les's phenomenal leadership style.

When Jerry had visited pastors' conferences on leadership, he just didn't see transparency. That bothered him. When people are transparent, they create accountability because they are making themselves vulnerable. That is what Les would do. Other leaders did the spin zone and cover-up. "One of the best things I learned from Les Ollila is that when I would introduce him I would say, one of the highest compliments that I could pay this man other than being a servant of God is simply this: with Les Ollila, you get no pretense, 24/7: what you see is what you get. If he would knock at this door at two in the morning or late at night, he would be the same man," testified Jerry. Those principles changed Jerry's life forever.

In Jerry's earnestness to follow Les and observe his ministry, he would enjoy the "napkin theology" sessions at the White Castle hamburger place in Roseville. The first time that they went there to talk, Jerry had never been to this place before. Les went up to the counter and ordered "one dozen with." Jerry thought, "This guy's getting a dozen hamburgers?" He didn't know that they were small and served on dinner-size rolls. He also didn't know that the "with" meant onions came on them all. Les Ollila was his hero, so he walked up to the counter and said, "one dozen with, too." Jerry cannot stand onions, but he sat there and gagged them down, all one dozen with onions just so he could have the privilege of talking to Les and getting some "napkin theology." Cheryl Hairgrove shared these thoughts: "So many today will give you three points and a poem and here are your problems, and here is what you need to do and go out and change, bye. Les always found a Bible parallel that was applicable to what you were going through." Jerry and Cheryl do not look at it as worshiping a man, but instead as recognizing a man who had the power of God on his life. His walk with God was obvious.

Still today, all of his kids from the Roseville days still affectionately refer to him as Uncle Les.

During his youth pastorate in Roseville, Les met someone who was to be a lifelong friend. Les always said that people all need a Paul, a Pal, and a Project. A Paul would be someone who is a mentor. A Pal is a buddy to laugh with. And a Project would be someone to care for and disciple in the Christian walk. A young man named Marty Von was going to Eastern Michigan University majoring in psychology and sociology in political science—double majoring.

Many of the pastors in the area went together to a camp in Brighton called *Camp of the Woods*. Some of them invited Marty to go, and there was going to be a golf outing that he could not resist, so he went. In the afternoon, he was told that there was going to be a counselor hunt for the campers. They needed adults to participate and so Marty, twenty-two years old, thought he could help them out and have a good time. He ran out into a field and found a patch of goldenrod and went to lie down in the field. Les Ollila came running into the field and had the same idea and nearly ran over him. They felt that now they would be too easy to find, so one of them suggested that they find another place to hide. They had never met before.

So they quickly introduced themselves and decided that an old junky deserted car would be the perfect spot. In the back seat of the car was a huge tarp. It was obviously filthy—dirty, dusty, and had been there forever. Marty tells the story: "We climbed in there on a hot summer day with the windows up to make everything look undisturbed, pulled the tarp over us and just were sweating and laughing together and chuckling over the fact that the campers would never think of that spot or would be afraid to open the car." It was their first meeting, but the result was a lifelong friendship. It never occurred to them that they could have run right into a hornet's nest or a home for snakes. Ah, the memories!

Marty got a part-time job working at a Christian radio station. In doing some advertising for the Christian radio station, there was a Bible institute that would announce classes, and Dr. Les Ollila was going to teach on the book of Acts. Les was youth pastor at Calvary of Roseville, and when Marty heard Les's name announced on the radio, he decided to take the study on the book of Acts. Les came over to the Bible institute on Monday nights to teach. Marty recalls the details of those days when he took classes with this endearing man whom he had met under a tarp as they hid from campers:

> *He was so interesting and unique and different as a speaker because this was the time when everyone was preaching no long hair and no short skirts. I did not hear Pastor Les, as everyone called him at the time, ever mention those things. He talked about a person's individual walk with the Lord and what your heart condition was because that will be lived through your life.*

Marty was also listening from a psychological standpoint that he was studying at the time. Marty had accepted Christ as Savior, but he was a non-committed believer. He was planning a career in professional baseball as he had already played semi-pro. As Marty went back to classes in the fall at Eastern Michigan to get his law degree first before going back to baseball, he was studying as part of his degree, Freudian psychology. He would go back to professors with Biblical truth that he had learned, but the college professors did not have answers for things that he would ask.

Marty's questions of Les were deeply psychological; Les always had a simple Biblical answer. This showed Marty wisdom and simplicity and yet a deep meaningful truth that intrigued him. After class at the Bible institute, Les would ask him to go out for coffee with him. "We were talking after class and he invited me to go to a shopping mall next to the large church where the institute was housed to go there for coffee. I didn't drink coffee, but I would go and drink tea or hot chocolate. He taught class from eight until ten and sometimes we would talk until midnight," Marty remembers. After those talks, Les would still have to drive an hour home, but Marty believes that casual discipleship with Biblical truths to life's questions redirected his life. It really drove Marty to the Bible to see what God was saying.

As their friendship developed, they would travel to sports clinics together. Les had played football and had run track in high school, and Marty had played semi-pro baseball; so they conducted pitching exhibitions for Christian groups and Les would have teen and parent seminars. Marty would be the pitcher and Les was the catcher for these exhibitions. During those days, *Leadership Ministries* was born. "L" for Les, and "M" for Marty made their ministry title significant. It seemed the name that God had given them. Marty worked out of a church on the western side of Detroit, and Les worked out of Calvary Baptist Church in Roseville, but they would come together often for these types of meetings to encourage leadership in homes and churches. The seeds were planted to begin a traveling team that would continue for the next thirty-plus years on the road with Life Action ministries and on still further to a Bible college setting. These two friends never would have dreamed that their *L and M* ministry would take the Christian world by storm.

CHAPTER TEN
LIFE ACTION ON THE ROAD

Be different on Purpose.

— Dr. Les Ollila

The heart behind *L and M* for Les and Marty and for *Leadership Ministries* began to influence hundreds across the United States in Christian circles. Marty Von remembers those days well:

> *When I ministered to the teens, he would minister to the adults and that's how Leadership Ministries was born. We decided that the most significant people that we could reach were the pastor as a leader and the father as a leader and a man in the family. Because our names began with L and M, we felt that God gave us the name for our ministry. While we were an hour apart and working out of different local churches, we would come together for these types of meetings.*

At the same time, a young evangelist, full of fervor and enthusiasm, had been leading a traveling ministry of teams that would spend two to three weeks in various churches in the United States and foreign countries, and they would bring encouragement and revival to these ministries everywhere. They were obviously being used of God. Eventually, Les and Marty were asked to fly across the country to join one team or another on a crusade, and they were to be the pastors for the team members. For these young people on these teams, constant traveling from ministry to ministry and church to church was not easy. Les and Marty had pastors' hearts, and they could counsel and advise the teams spiritually.

The Life Action Ministries with Evangelist Del Fehsenfeld came to Marty's church one time. This was a meeting where Marty surrendered his life to love and serve God. Marty had a burden to see the United States spiritually revived, probably in part because of his political science drive with its wide scope. Del was looking for a few men that had burdens for revival, so Marty recommended Les to Del. So began their connections with Life Action Ministry. God was expanding Del's ministry to a national dimension, so this was an exciting time to jump on board.

Once a month, Les and Marty would travel wherever Life Action teams were holding meetings, and they would minister with them. The evangelistic meetings included sessions where pastors were trained in ministry philosophy, where families in churches were trained in Biblical philosophies of the home, and where an evangelistic outreach permeated the church and the community. The last couple nights of the meetings were reaching out to the surrounding neighborhood with the Gospel. As Life Action teams solidified their course in those early days, it was Dr.

Ollila that set the rudder for the man, Del Fehsenfeld, and the ministry, Life Action.

Les slowly phased out of his youth pastorate with the Roseville church, but he had aptly trained youth sponsors to take over the work, and the older teens as well led the group very efficiently. Pastor Rhodes was unselfish enough to see that Les had a burden with a scope that reached national boundaries. Les had a consuming passion to get a message out to people. His love for others and helping others drove him onward. So Pastor Rhodes tried to encourage him all the way.

As Les's ministry increased with the Life Action teams, his responsibilities became increasingly abundant. Del Fehsenfeld was the evangelist really driving the crusades, but Les and Marty were pastoring the teams themselves; each team had team leaders, and then the teams themselves were made up college and career-aged young adults with a heart for God. Marty Herron recalls the early days with Les: "His willingness to spend time that was not in the pulpit and not in any teaching or preaching scenario characterized his ministry. He communicated with you that 'I care about you and I want to be with you.'" Life Action provided an atmosphere conducive to God's having a great reign in the hearts of men. It was not canned revival or showmanship as it is in many cases today on television. In those days, the Life Action teams really became bonded. The closeness was that of family, security, and friendship.

Wynne Kimbrough, one of the leaders of the teams, remembers meeting Les for the first time. The team Wynne was with were in Kansas, and they found out that Del wanted them in Maryland in a matter of two days to begin a meeting there. Circumstances had demanded that the team travel quickly to do this. Wynne was eighteen years old at the time. The team arrived in Maryland rung out. This is the first thing Wynne remembers Doc. O saying: "'When we are weak, He is strong'. Les knew the need of the team—physically weak and needing to be spiritually alert. I was young and immature, and I can remember thinking, 'Sure?' Yet the Lord is faithful and it is true and the Lord helped us. It was my first exposure to Les." Wynne traveled with the Life Action Ministries for ten years. For one full year, Les was his team pastor. Wynne traveled the nine remaining with Marty Von as his team pastor.

Every day the team would have a meeting with Les. He would also meet with the team after supper. They would pray together, and he was always available to counsel any one of the team members. Les preached for the family seminar times, and he would conduct leadership seminars as well in the various churches. Then on Thursdays and Fridays, Les would lead a youth seminar called *Master Control.* He would teach half or more of the lessons each week to the teens. Then on a daily basis as well, he would meet with Del and the pastor of the church staff and go over leadership principles and personal walk with God. The whole focus was not only to revive the church, but it was a mini-discipleship time for all involved. Wynne comments: "Not to be melodramatic, but it was like the prophets that would come and be used of God to stir up the people. That was the function of the crusade ministry."

The teams and Del himself developed a deep love for Les Ollila. They respected him highly. One time Wynne remembers Del saying something interesting after Les had finished ministering with Life Action; he said that the wisdom that God had given Les as a young man was overwhelming. He said that he wished that Les could come and just stand up in front without saying a word for forty-five minutes and kids would look at him. He wouldn't even have to say a word for him to influence those young people. Dr. Ollila laid much of the foundation of what Life Action Crusades are about even to today.

One thing that he was known for in a humorous way with many pastors across the United States was his "napkin theology" and his transparencies that he used all the time. Les couldn't explain anything to people personally unless he could write on a napkin; and in speaking to a crowd, he always used an overhead transparency. In the mid-70's that was innovative technology, so it really stuck in their minds. He became known as "Les Overlay."

As a family, during the crusades, the Ollilas would travel in an air stream trailer called, "The Silver Pickle." Les would want to drive his own rig because of his love for driving big machinery and such. But he was always willing to drive whatever equipment they needed. He had no image of himself like "I need someone else to serve me." Les was part of the team and he did practical things and mundane things and never gave the impression that he wanted to be served.

For the children, the travels were a busy, exciting time. Lisa (Ollila) Swanson recalls those days on the road with Life Action:

> *What I remember was packing up and taking off from Roseville. And we would go—we did not see my dad except for every night at 5 o'clock, but he would counsel until all hours in the morning. He would get up early and be gone meeting with pastors. It was a good experience for me because I became out-going. We would go into a church and people would not come up and talk to you. You had to go up to them. I could talk to anybody and I would make lots of friends.*

So even though her family would be busy when they traveled on the road, Lisa felt that the positive side of that was the result of opening up and learning how to talk to and to meet complete strangers.

Tami's memories with the Life Action focused on other more dramatic experiences. She recalls that they encountered several tornadoes especially when they would travel in Texas. Tami has always seen her dad as a man of faith and prayer. He always taught the children God's provision, protection, and power. One storm really has remained in Tami's memories:

> *I remember that we had been in the state of Texas for a while. And we hit a lot of storms in Texas and I think that is where it was for sure. We saw a tornado coming, turned and ran into the church and we dropped to our knees and my dad huddled his arms around us and we prayed and he said, "God, you must protect us." We looked up and that tornado jumped right over the church. It was unbelievable. That made the biggest impression on me as a child. It gives me the chills to talk about it.*

The team members always made the children part of the family. The children attended the Happiness Club or the Dynamite Club where the team members would excitedly teach during the regular services. The team members used puppets or ventriloquism or any number of other creative presentations.

One more very vivid memory for the family was a special answer to prayer. They had a pressing need for a vehicle that was adequate for all of the constant traveling that they did. They prayed for God to provide—this was the only way that Les knew to handle the need. The children remember praying day after day specifically for a Ford Van with captain's chairs. When God answered that prayer, it was very specific. A family asked the Ollilas if they needed a vehicle, and that was the exact van that they gave to the family. So they drove away in their captain's seats. Les's faith has been great over the years.

Dr. Ollila's vision for revival for the nation drove Les and still drives him today. Life Action was a vehicle for Les to share with a nation. He believes that God is a powerful God that could bring revival to America and the Holy Spirit could work. Today, this continues to be an emphasis of his. Many people look at this possibility with dismay, but Les, even though he is a realist, believes that God could change this nation if He were to work and His Holy Spirit were to touch the United States. Les persists in doing his part to bring that to fruition.

Chapter Eleven
Transitions North

If you know Him, yielding to Him is natural.

— Dr. Les Ollila

At this point in Les's life after having been in the ministry at Bootleg Corner, and then in Roseville, and then in Life Action where he led many leadership conferences and spoke in many parent seminars, he was in great demand in Christian ministry. After concluding his active part in the Life Action teams, he settled back into Roseville for about one year. He liked Roseville, and he liked Calvary. He liked the people; he liked to work with Pastor Rhodes, and Pastor Rhodes liked to work with him. But just the same as when he went on the road with Life Action, God was not giving him complete rest. He told Pastor Rhodes that he needed to go, but he did not know where. He could not imagine the task that would be placed before him. He had several offers for positions across the country, some very lucrative, but he was not specifically directed to take any one position.

Meanwhile, events were unfolding in the little town of Dunbar in northern Wisconsin that would point Les and his family back north. God had made his instrument a man named Paul Patz, an immigrant Polish farmer with a third grade education, to begin a small camp on Dunbar property in 1961. Paul's inventions made him a wealthy man, and he wanted to put that wealth back into ministry. Then in

1976 the Northland Mission, Inc. started a Bible Institute that blossomed into a Bible College by the very next year. Marty Herron, Les and Charlene's dear friends from Life Action, had moved north to direct Northland Camp. Marty and Tami had been attending a camp director's institute for six months when Harold Patz, son of Paul Patz, founder of Northland Mission, Inc. called the institute to see if they had a couple that they could recommend to the position of camp director in Dunbar. Marty and Tami flew up to Dunbar, Wisconsin, in November and agreed to come on board. They flew home, packed up their little old Robin's Egg Blue Volkswagen beetle and drove up to Dunbar on the coldest day of winter in December of 1981. In 1982, they ran their first summer camps for five weeks and had four hundred individual campers and twenty families attend. Marty wanted some good speakers lined up for the next summer, so he called his buddies, Les Ollila and Marty Von, who consented to come to speak. Amazingly enough, Les had actually visited the camp in Dunbar when the Patz family organized the camp in its fledging years. So he was familiar with "out-of-the-way Dunbar." The administrative council consisting of Bill Arndt, Ernie Schmidt, John Littleton, and Jim Morgenroth realized that the school needed a college president because they had gone for four years without a president. Harold Patz and Marty Herron lived on the Northland campus in duplexes. They were neighbors. After Les preached one night, the next day,

Harold was talking to Marty at their screen doors on the back porch, and they were both wondering if Les would be willing to come as president for the Bible College.

Marty recalls some of those days clearly: "I thought, 'That would be great,' but I didn't know if he would come and if he would be comfortable in the educational setting, but I said, 'Call him.'" He recommended that they first call Pastor Rhodes because Les was presently under him and they needed to talk to Pastor first. Bob Rhodes thought that Les would be perfect. So they called Les to ask him if he would consider it. Pastor Rhodes remembers Les getting the call: "I encouraged him in every way. I said, 'Les, you have the ability—here's an opportunity for you to put your life into many, many other lives.'" It was that conversation and those unselfish encouraging words that caused Les to consider this path before him.

During the summer of 1983, when Les first came up to Northland in an official speaking capacity, a bunch of the faculty guys played touch football. Jim Bennett and "Tyke" (Will) Arndt, twelve-year-olds at the time, were a part of that neighborhood ritual along with Harold Patz and various other adults and faculty kids. Dr. Ollila came over to play in his old tattered sweat pants that had a huge tear in them. He looked like one of the boys. Will Arndt turned and whispered to Jim, "I think that guy is here to interview for the presidency of the college." He was "cool" to the kids, but an adult surely would have done a double take. There was not a pretentious bone in his body. There never had been and there never would be.

As Les and Marty Von had traveled together from 1968 to the present 1983, they had often spoken of fleshing out their philosophies of leadership training in a Bible college setting, but they would joke, "Who would have us?" Initially, as Harold Patz approached Les, Les said that he would be delighted to teach in the Bible department and just be part of the team. But the board of directors was impressed with Les, loving his down-to-earth nature and his walk with God. Papa Patz, Harold's dad, the president of the board at that time, fell in love with Les immediately. As Dr. Les Ollila worked things through in his mind and heart, he spent many hours walking the campus of Northland that summer and praying for God's direction. When Les was able to hear Paul Patz's testimony of how he was directed by the Lord to begin Northland Ministry, Les knew there and then that this was the vision that he wanted to be a part of. He just wanted to ride the coat tails of this godly man, Paul Patz. Paul was a man who had little education, had had twenty-five surgeries on his mouth for cancer, but who gave his life and money to meet the needs of young people in the camp setting and Bible College campus. Northland provided a venue where Les could invest his time in hundreds of students, and he could invest in future leadership concentrated for four years rather than run from meeting to meeting around the country as he had been doing for a long time.

Dr. Ollila moved his family up north in the spring of 1984 and Marty Von moved into his duplex in August of the same year. Les did a lot of observing of the college functions from April of 1984 until the fall of 1984. Enrollment at the college had risen to as high as 150 students in 1980, but that number had begun to decline. So Les was a key with all of his contacts to help bring a known name to the campus to bring attention to what Northland was doing. It was just the difference that the administrative council and the board of directors needed.

Harold Patz remembers those early college days:

> *Everything was like Sam Drucker's General Store. It was a bottle neck in the dining hall. All of the offices for Northland were there. The administration and staff were utilizing much of the dining hall for their offices and facilities. There were two white dorms for the students and the chapel was built across the way to complete the main campus in those days. In 1979 a men's dorm was built so the guys were moved over there. In 1976 they built the first library on campus and in 1978 a gym was built for the recreation for the students. The next ladies' dorm was built in the later 80's.*

Some terrific changes were taking place as Les, the Martys, and Harold Patz worked to see changes of philosophy and direction especially from 1984 through 1986. They rewrote the student handbook to reflect their philosophies of servant leadership. Harold shared these words: "Les really helped us establish a good name because he had a good name. We became, 'Oh that's where Dr. Ollila is.' So it also made it easier to recruit staff. Many people knew him—he was youth pastor, or people heard him in conventions for years. People wanted to come where he was." His simple "non-big-shot" personality was magnetic. As an administrator, he always involved the entire team on decision-making. He was more of a coach, and his team loved him and followed his leadership. Les's heart was to help the little people—the struggling pastors—the young people with a heart for missions or the pastorate. This was perfect for him.

Dr. Ernie Schmidt, one of the members of the administrative board did a one-year evaluation on the presidency of Les. The following are excerpts of that report: I sense personal spiritual growth as a result of his life and ministry. The individual making that kind of impact is Dr. Leslie Ollila, the "new" president of Northland Baptist Bible College, Dunbar, Wisconsin. In just a year, God has used him to make a significant impact on the lives of staff and students alike. His ministry has added a new dimension to the atmosphere of the college known as "the Northland spirit."

Les, as he is known by friends (or Dr. O., as he is affectionately referred to by students), is one who can be characterized by the phrase, "down-to-earth." He is genuine and transparent. He is a friend who makes you "feel at home" with his informal and humorous personality. Although his personality is commendable, his real strength lies in his character. Anyone who spends time with him or hears him speak realizes he is a man of the Word and prayer. Meditation on Scripture and obedience have made Biblical principles and a Biblical philosophy an integral part of his life. Thus, Northland is not only becoming the reflection of a man, but of a man of God.

As he looks back over those early years [of his life], two things stand out as being life-changing. First, there were friends who took an interest in him and helped and encouraged him spiritually. Secondly, he remembers three plaques in [Hart's] home that were indelibly impressed upon his mind. One was the familiar saying, "Only one life, 'twill soon be past. Only what is done for Christ will last." Another was Jim Elliot's quote, "A man is no fool to give up that which he cannot keep to gain that which he cannot lose." The third was the challenging statement, "Only that is important which is eternal."

[Here at Northland] Dr. Ollila had as his aim training individuals with "a heart for God" a phrase that he uses consistently. He had three specific goals as he assumed his responsibilities: (1) to establish the unity of a single heartbeat concerning the direction of the school among the faculty; (2) to bring the students to the place of manifesting a rejoicing and submissive spirit; and (3) to maintain an outreach ministry off campus. After the first year, these goals are being realized.

How has it been? With the faculty and staff, Les has shown himself a friend and an example. One of his characteristic sayings is, "Leadership is not lordship, but servitude." His life is an incarnation of that statement. Thus, his staff respects him. By personal contact and in staff meetings, he invests his life and philosophy in his fellow workers. Because of his depth of insight in the Word and his walk with God, his chapel ministry is a source of challenge and growth to faculty as well as students. Hence, both his private life and public ministry are building a staff with a unified heart. Dr. Ollila's ministry with the students is a sharing of his life and burden with the view of seeing present spiritual growth and equipping them for the future. Under his leadership, Northland has incorporated personal devotions into the daily schedule. The purpose is not to try to legislate holiness, but to seek to enable the students to establish a life pattern of beginning the day with God. Obviously, he does want them to benefit from it on a daily basis. It is his desire that they not only know the Word of God, but that they also see the works of God in their lives. He believes a consistent time with God will enable them to experience God's working in their lives and thus, have a consistent "current" testimony.

His emphasis this past year has been in two words, honesty and obedience. The honesty encouraged was not merely being truthful in speech, but being honest with God when convicted of sin and being transparent with others. The emphasis on obedience was that of responding immediately to the Word and the promptings of the Holy Spirit. This emphasis is beginning to be reflected in the lives of students in their relationship to God and others.

Dr. Ollila's informal, unassuming, and winsome approach in conversation and preaching often has the students "eating out of his hand." He utilizes the charisma to build them up, not for personal ends. Students know this and, consequently, are beginning to respond to the Lord, through his ministry, with a rejoicing and submissive spirit. Hence, he is seeing his second goal in progress of fulfillment.

There are many more demands for Dr. Ollila to minister outside the college than he can fulfill. His third goal is, thus, fulfilled. This also, presents abundant motivation for him to keep his focus on the overall goal of training staff and future leaders with the burden God has given him. These demands consistently remind him that others must be sent out "with his heart" to minister where he cannot.

In the future, Dr. Ollila wants to intensify his present goals to train students to be others-centered in life and ministry. This desire is not just to train them to be experts in interpersonal relationships (though that is a goal), but to prepare them to serve others effectively from a solid doctrinal foundation. His concern is, hence, that students have a firm grasp of the Bible and other subjects that will make them effective in communicating the truth in a meaningful and Godly manner.

He believes this will be accomplished through his ministry and the staff. He knows a faculty, right with God, who are not only teaching, but also training by one-on-one discipleship will present a proper role-model for the students. Thus, his desire is that he and the staff be what God wants them to be so they can do what He wants them to do. In this type of ministry, truth is not only taught, but Godly lives are reproduced. In other words, the students will not only be taught, but they will be trained for God's service.

Dr. Ollila states that three factors make up a Christian college: facilities, faculty, and focus. As in all other institutions, Northland has facilities and faculty. He shares his desire to see the good facilities and faculty at Northland be used of God to give the right focus. That focus is to help build Biblical life patterns as a basis for learning. The end result will be Christian leaders who are trained to handle the Word of God effectively and lead with a servant's spirit.

I predict that, as the Lord tarries and by God's enablement, Dr. Ollila's life will be used to influence many to minister in that manner "with a heart for God" (Schmidt, "After"1–8).

Almost prophetically, the enrollment went from 125 in the fall of 1984 to 179 in the fall of 1986. Dr. Schmidt's prediction continues to come true. In 2003, Dr. O's ministry blesses over 700 students.

But the next chapter in the life of the Ollilas was going to be one of deep valleys and rocky pathways. One afternoon in the spring of 1987, Les and Charlene's boy, Steven, was playing at a neighbor's house. Steven's buddy's dad had a "cool" knife collection. They were looking at the knives and one began to fall to the floor and out of instinct, Steven reached for the knife to keep it from falling to the floor completely. Steven ended up slicing his wrist. The Ollilas took him up to the hospital to have Steven's hand checked and have it cleaned up and bound.

The next day, Steven went to school and he started to feel very ill. But like any other parent told something similar, his folks thought that it was an excuse to come home, so they told him that he would be fine until the end of the day. They knew something was drastically wrong when the usually "bouncing-off-the-walls" Steven came home and collapsed on the couch. When they unwound his bandages from his wrist, they were shocked to see that serious infection had set in. It was not just the normal staph infection that he had contracted, but he had picked up a much more serious infection while he had been up at the hospital. Steven was admitted into the hospital immediately and the doctors were extremely concerned as to whether they could save Steven's arm and even if they could save his life. Les and Charlene were faced with this news, and the next few days were crucial. The antibiotics given intravenously were not taking effect and Steven grew worse by the hour. Either Les or Charlene was with him constantly.

Everyone was praying back on campus for Steven and his condition. When doctors at the Iron Mountain hospital discovered that his second strain of infectious bacteria was much stronger than they had first thought, they began a much more high-powered treatment. Finally, after several days, Steven began to get better. Les spent many hours by his side and begged God to spare Steven's life. As Steven recuperated, he started to go stir-crazy and figured out a way to use his hospital paraphernalia to make a ball and glove; and hour after hour he would toss his ball against the wall. He was ready to go home.

Simultaneous with this crisis, Les and Charlene were facing yet another series of "valley-days." Here it was their first years at Northland and they were being turned inside out with busyness and trial upon trial. Lisa, Les and Char's oldest girl, was seventeen at the time in this spring of 1987. She hadn't shared her news with anyone until it was inevitable that she must tell her parents. Charlene took her up to the hospital for a test. She indeed was pregnant.

Les was about to "kick" the whole presidency loose and head back to the woods of the UP. When it first came out, Les had a meeting with the entire faculty, staff, and student body. Everyone gathered in the white chapel in the center of campus.

Les's approach was, "This is my failure, not Lisa's. I've blown it." He felt like he had been too busy traveling and he had not been there for Lisa. Lisa was very sorry for hurting her folks, and everyone could see their brokenness. When Les took the approach of being transparent rather than hiding and covering up, he was far greater of a blessing to those who worked with him. He felt the weight of the fact that he had traveled all these years sharing with people in leadership conferences and he was wondering about his own leadership in his own home. However, many godly pastors and leaders around the country and the Northland board of directors themselves encouraged him to stay on as president, and people were loving enough to encourage instead of criticize. Les even went to the neighbors surrounding Northland's campus and was very open about what the Ollilas were going through at that time. Les and Charlene and Lisa decided that Les and Charlene would raise the baby. And so John David became a part of the family. Lisa relates her feelings:

> *I agreed to that. And I guess it is the best thing. John doesn't ever want to leave there [Les and Charlene's home]. That is his life. It's hard for me.*

I love John and whatever makes him happy. A lot of people judge. He has a better life; he's able to do more. My dad is a very good father. I'm not about to interfere. John David is sweet and he is lucky. He has really loved my mom and dad.

Interestingly enough, the enrollment went up dramatically that fall. In the fall of 1986 there were 167 students, and in the fall of 1987 the enrollment jumped to 243 (Harder, Anna). What would explain this? One would think that enrollment would drop when the president of a Bible college has a daughter get pregnant out of wedlock. But people who were hurting saw a man who was hurting and they were attracted to the way he handled himself and his family with honesty and transparency in days of trials. Sometimes his trials were of more concern to others than to himself.

Another way he keeps his sanity when facing problems perhaps on a more mundane level in the ministry is with humor. Generally, that is how he tends to deal with difficulties in the ministry. Dr. O has never been about following tangents and exterior-forced spirituality. People in the ministry can be so petty at times. Pastors have called him about such silly things over the years. Tami recalls one instance:

My dad is a focused person. One time I was in his office and Gen Schmidt was my dad's secretary.

And she said, "Dr. Ollila, I have this letter that this pastor has written and I don't think that we can avoid it any longer. He keeps calling." He wanted to know my dad's biblical stand on Santa Claus. I remember my dad's answer meant whether or not this pastor would send his students here to school. My dad is not easily swayed by people's threats or political gains. Well, my dad is looking at it saying, "This is so petty." All of the problems that he is making decisions about and he gets this. I remember sitting and wondering, "What's my dad going to do?" I remember thinking that. I looked at Gen and my dad turned around he said, "Genevieve, tell the man that I think Santa is a very kind jolly old plump man who has been very good to me over the years." That was his answer. Gen said, "You are kidding?" And he said, "Nope—that's my answer." I don't know if she sent it, but that was his final answer.

That really stayed with Tami. Her dad was not about petty things. Politicking didn't sway him. He kept his focus on his goals and he refused to play the games of tangents and petty problems. By the way, the letter did not get sent.

Not only did God test the Ollilas with the lives of Steven and the decision that Lisa made, but they also had to face another test in the life of Tami. Jim Bennett and Tami had married in 1992. Jim was the son of one of the long-time faculty members, Dr. Doug Bennett. Jim and Tami had been friends through high school, and then they dated throughout their college years. In 1996, Jim and Tami found out they were expecting their first child. All the joys that come along with that news were theirs and the family's. They both thought that with this bliss came a perfectly healthy pregnancy and baby to follow. This is only natural for any couple expecting a baby for the first time. God prepared Tami in a special way for what she was about to face. She said to Jim one day, "Jim, something is wrong, and I don't think that I will deliver this baby." Jim tried to comfort her doubts, but indeed she was correct when by the fourth month they still hadn't heard the heartbeat. The doctor did further testing, and the pregnancy was a molar pregnancy. The baby was growing at the end of the placenta, and a mole grew as well taking the nutrition from the child. The baby died at two or three months into the pregnancy.

Further testing showed that the center of the mole looked cancerous. Tami had to go through blood testing twice a week and go in for blood work as often. The doctors performed a D and C because sometimes these pregnancies can last a full-term. So, Jim and Tami went to a clinic in Marshfield. Tami had special cancer testing there and she had to go back every couple months to have further testing. Tami told Jim:

> *This is sometimes the hardest when you have to wait on God not knowing the answers and you have to trust. But even if it is cancer, I have to trust, too. It was hard for me to come to that point, but when I got there, I was fine. I struggled, and honestly, I struggled a lot. You question God—this is our first baby. I said to God, "You've got to help me because I do not understand." Finally I came to the point where I said, "OK, God, you are in control and I just trust you even if it's bad."*

Les and Charlene struggled as well through these days with Jim and Tami. Les reminded Tami of God's goodness through it all and that God is sovereign in His choices. One year later, Jim and Tami did give birth to a beautiful, healthy daughter, Tori. God's goodness was given back to them in this special gift. So, God ran Les and Charlene through another grid of trial and test. They were consistent and they trusted God that He knew what was best for all of them.

On a typical Monday morning, Doc O. will stand in the chapel hour and lead the student body in some singing and then a "works of God" time together. His winning and warm ways command an audience as he loves to hear of the many ways that students see God at work in their lives. A typical testimony would include such examples as a young lady speaking into the roving microphone about how she needed fifteen hundred dollars for her bill and how God supplied in a miraculous way. Another scenario would be a young man perhaps sharing how he had an opportunity on an extension ministry to lead someone to Christ. Yet another would be the story of how people's prayers sustained a young person through a tragic family death. People that visit the campus seem to remark concerning two observations: the students' friendly family atmosphere that they create and the heartthrob of the school—the servant spirit. Dr. Ollila has rubbed that off from the core of his being. That is what makes him tick. That is what he dreamed would be the overwhelming sense on a Christian college campus that he would lead.

One sidelight, which absolutely cannot be left out, is his superhero status as the campus "Duct-tape Man." This started a few years back when he put duct tape on his wallet to hold it together. He and Charlene were down in Green Bay at a store. As they came out of the store, they saw a couple struggling to get large items into their car. Not untypical, Les and Charlene were the first ones over to help. When they completed the job, the couple asked for his business card. He pulled out his duct-taped wallet and opened it and gave them the card. Well, in chapel a week later, he proudly displayed the new wallet that this lady had sent to him because she felt sorry for him. Over the next few weeks, he then displayed a duct-taped Bible cover that one of the students had made for him. Soon to follow were a duct-taped ball cap, duct-taped shoes, and finally, rivaling all other duct-taped items, a suit coat that one student had meticulously made entirely from duct-tape. Dr. Ollila, as unpretentious as he is, wore the suit coat for commencement practice in the spring of 2002. Faculty members have future plans to make him duct-tape ties and duct-tape slippers and duct-tape brief cases. He really likes his broken-in duct-tape wallet; so when he travels, he wears his finest suit, puts in ***fake*** rotten false teeth, and pulls out his wallet for an upgrade on his frequent-flyer miles, and he loves to see the reactions of the airline employees. After traveling so much, his airline employee friends in Green Bay, Wisconsin, never know what to expect when he approaches the counter.

With all of his fun and "down-home" style of leadership, Dr. Ollila's influence over Northland in the years that followed cannot be overstated. He gave nearly 20 years of his life to thousands of young adults. Dr. Jim Bennett (Dean of Education at Northland) wrote a dissertation including in part the life of Paul Patz, the founder of Northland. He stated about that work, "I felt like there were two people that you really needed to know to understand Northland—Papa Patz and Dr. Ollila because they were so influential. I don't think that you can overstate leadership. Everyone is important in the institution but he is greatly influential. He has set the rudder for philosophy and direction."

Northland board, faculty, staff, and alumni speak for themselves as to the influence of Dr. O:

Our college and ministry was struggling in the early 1980's with its direction and leadership. Our enrollment in the college was shrinking rather than growing. We thank God that He led us to Dr. Les Ollila who set the rudder and who modeled true servant leadership. His personal discipleship, his genuine transparency, and his constant example of living for others first has touched this board and has shaped Northland Mission, Inc. **[Howard Patz, chairman of the board for Northland Mission, Inc. speaking on behalf of the board]**

When I first met Doc O, my heart was knit to his. Here was God's man, His humble servant, so selfless, so abandoned to Christ, so full of genuine spiritual life. His life was and is so intensely focused on what really matters for eternity. It is now my great privilege to be mentored by him and to labor with him as we prepare this next generation of servant-leaders for Great Commission living. **[Dr. Matt Olson, president of Northland Baptist Bible College]**

Dr. Ollila is comfortable speaking to both kings and paupers. I've been with Dr. O when we have gone to NBA games, and I've seen Dr. O on the court talking with Michael Jordan; and he's got Michael

Jordan laughing. And I'm saying how did he get down there? Much less, how is he doing that? I've seen him with dignitaries, congressmen, and the President. His comfort level is broad; I think that is what makes him so usable by the Lord because he ministers to everyone. You may be a four star general, but you may be Bill Smith; or you may be knee deep in farm chores. He's comfortable on all levels and he is the same. That is God-given. **[Dr. Jim Bennett, Dean of Education at Northland Baptist Bible College]**

I think there is one thing that shows his character—in a way he is like Papa Patz—he may not have had all of the operations with all of the cancer that Papa had, but Les has had tremendous physical difficulties over the years and headaches all of the time, but he keeps going. **[Professor Jerry Fair, Elementary Education Instructor]**

What you see is what you get. He doesn't pretend to be more than he is: willing to do anything. He has never put on airs of a big shot. He's president of a college, but how many presidents get out and drive pay loaders or get in trucks to help you with menial tasks. He's a person who has always been willing to do something. He doesn't like hypocrisy. He doesn't like people to be something that they are not. Once the ministry is producing others who have that kind of a servant attitude to those who need it—that's how I would characterize him. **[Dr. Doug Bennett, Theology Instructor and Library Supervisor]**

He is not concerned with climbing the ladder of success or being recognized. He is just as quick to talk to a student or child as he is the President of the United States. This quality of humility has been a great challenge and blessing to me. It is one thing to preach a life lesson—Doc O lives his life lessons. His commitment to God and his work have made a profound impact in my life. **[Josh Beers, Northland Graduate]**

I have to say that next to my mother and father, Les was truly the man whose example helped me remain faithful during many crises in ministry and family. Memories of his spirit and attitude still motivate me as I serve in this challenging [counseling] ministry. Les Ollila's genuineness, humility, and apolitical approach to serving God, not men, have been a blessing in my life that words cannot express. I truly think of him as a second father. **[Jim Phillips, Former faculty member and coach]**

He has modeled to me the servant-leadership example; he always took time to share a cup of coffee; he never seemed rushed even when I know he had more important things waiting. Dr. Ollila wasn't untouchable; he has had problems like all of us, but he has been transparent about them and that kind of honesty in ministry is greatly needed. We love him. **[Les Heinze, Doctor of Ministries Graduate]**

His down-to-earth personality has allowed the Northland ministry to be just like home. **[Andy Rupert, Northland Graduate]**

One of the most imparting aspects of Dr. Ollila's ministry has been his passion for discipleship and Great Commission living. I'll never forget sitting in a staff meeting during my first year at Northland and hearing Doc O say, "We are not an educational institution trying to make disciples; we are a disciple-making institution first and we use education as a means to accomplish this goal." Many others have adequately described this passion in the chapters of this book. However, I speak to this as one who came later in his ministry life and found his burden for discipleship went beyond teens or students. One of the primary ways his life impacted mine was the extended time spent together over years of traveling together. Traveling with Doc is never dull and many "discipleship moments" surface on almost every trip. Travel is an exhausting necessity associated with college administration. On one occasion Dr. Ollila, Dr. Von, and I were flying out to the same conference together. It had been a particularly heavy travel time and we were all exhausted. As he took his seat next to Marty in the row ahead of me, Doc 0 expressed what Marty and I were thinking. In a not too subtle voice he began observing "I must have a sickness or a disease. Honest Marty, every time I see an airport I have to get in a Northwest plane!" The man sitting next to me was doing his best not to laugh aloud. He leaned over and whispered, "Can you believe this guy?" I was already trying to keep from laughing and his comment pushed me past the point of reasonable self-control. I have on many occasions seen Doc take out his Bible on a flight and it won't be too long before his seatmates or flight attendants will ask him if they can talk. On more than a few occasions, we will learn upon landing that he had the privilege of leading someone to Christ. Observing this in him has been a powerful reminder and encouragement to make sure that I am striving to live for the Great Commission myself. **[Dr. Sam Horn, Executive**

Vice President of Northland Baptist Bible College]

Finally, the story that follows sums up what Dr. Ollila has been all about throughout his years of modeling someone who loves people and gives of himself:

> *Last year at my commencement, a friend of mine came to see me graduate. I was very concerned for this young man's soul. This friend of mine had struggled with drugs; he had long hair and "grunge" clothing. I know he felt uncomfortable as I left him alone while I returned my cap and gown. When I came back, I saw Dr. Ollila with his arm around him, talking to him and taking the time to be a friend. I am sure by that time, my friend did not smell very nice (as he had on long sleeves to hide his scars), and he was extremely shy as well. I was so awed by the fact that this man who was so definitely wanted by so many people would take the time to show God's love to my friend who struggled with drugs. Thank you, Dr. Ollila, for showing me real-life Christianity. I love you.* **[Rebekah Drake, Northland Graduate]**

"Transitions North" turned into almost twenty years of touching lives worldwide. September 23rd, 2002 marked the changing of the guard. President Matt Olson stepped into Les's position as president of Northland at a very emotionally stirring ceremony, and Les became the chancellor of the college. Les's influence will continue as Dr. Olson has expressed that he is here to hold up the arms of Les and to learn from him. Dr. Ollila plans to continue his ministry with faculty, staff, and students; Dr. Ollila hopes to put his philosophies into writing.

Chapter Twelve
August 18th, 2001, and the Days That Followed

God owns me, and I am not free to choose my own way.

— Dr. Les Ollila

Sam, Marty, Les, and John David got off the plane in Green Bay and went to the baggage claim, and still no one said anything to anyone. Would Charlene be alive—what would the news be that greeted them there? Harold Patz and Tim Corey met them at the airport. Susan Von was there as well, and she reported that Charlene was alive and in surgery. Susan, Marty, and Sam had another prayer meeting right there and then. Marty took the time to tell John David the gravity of the situation. John David responded well, and Marty was glad that he could tell JD that his mom was still alive. Marty still knew that he did not know the full extent of the seriousness of the situation. Marty asked John David to pray, and Marty himself prayed as well.

When they got to the hospital, the waiting room was full of friends and relatives—mostly friends from Northland. Marty Von tried to stay by the door where the doctors would come out from the surgery. Lisa shared that it was a bit awkward seeing her dad for the first time in a room full of people. Tami said she could see in her dad's eyes when he arrived at the hospital the question of whether Charlene was indeed alive or dead. We all assured him. "She is still here. She is in surgery; she is alive but it is very touch and go." Les gathered the children together and went into a private room.

Lisa and Brian, Tami and Jim, Steven and Danae, John David, and Les sat together in the privacy of a room adjacent to the waiting room outside surgery. He said that he and Charlene had prayed for intimacy with God and they didn't know what God would use in their lives to draw them to Him. Les never dreamed that God would touch Charlene's life. He was honest with them all and told them that he wanted to see changes in all of their lives; and if this was the way God had chosen to bring that about, so be it. Then they went to prayer and there were few words that could be spoken. Their hearts' groanings were the only sounds in the room.

One of the surgical assistants came out of the operating room and reported to Marty Von that Mrs. Ollila had made it through a difficult surgery, an operation rarely performed because patients usually never make it to the operating table. They were finishing suturing her. So while Marty had the difficulty of sharing the tragic news initially to Les at the Minneapolis airport, he had the joy of weeping and telling of his thankfulness to God for how far she had come and that she was still alive.

Lisa assessed the whole picture as the physicians related that they had to go into Char's back and break their mom's ribs to get to the aorta. They couldn't promise several things. The operation had been done in such haste that they felt there might be brain damage, paralysis, or any number of side-effects. They truly didn't know if she would live through recovery. Her blood pressure was an urgent issue. Doctors had to get that down because it was 215 or 220 still. Lisa shared, "And then my dad thanked the doctor and told him that we are Christians and that we had a lot of people praying." Then they went in to see her and she looked very swollen and not like herself at all. That was probably the hardest moment for John David throughout the ordeal.

As Charlene recovered slowly over the coming days in the hospital and at home, the Northland family went to work round the clock with people cleaning, making meals, sitting with Charlene, running errands, and just being available. Of course, prayer was continuing constantly for the family. The most glaring side-effect of Charlene's ordeal was that she had lost her voice. In the doctor's haste to operate, apparently he thought that he may have severed a nerve that had a connection to the voice box. Her efforts to speak came out as high-pitched squeals and squeaks. The physicians told Charlene that if her voice did not return within six months, it never would. No one cared what she sounded like. Everyone was so glad to see her alive and recovering. Les said in one meeting, "I don't care if she flails her arms and can never speak again, I am so thrilled to have her with me."

Her first day back in church many months after the surgery was not only a time of rejoicing for all of the immediate Ollila family, but it was a time of rejoicing for Northland's family also. The holidays take on a new meaning, and every time Les walks through the door of their house and sees Charlene sitting there, he says that he will never take that for granted. Additionally, God did another miracle in her life: after several months of vocal therapy, Charlene's normal voice returned. To this day, Charlene is almost back to normal with extreme fatigue being the only nuisance.

Les and Charlene are a dear couple who have faced unique trials and walked through the fires and floods victoriously. Les has always said that if a man would be used greatly, God must hurt him deeply. Les Ollila, a man who stands in the gap, has made a mark on people's hearts for all eternity. He stands out as **a man among them—a man among men.**

Afterwords

He has been a consistent man throughout all of his trials.

— Wynne Kimbrough

He is a model of a man who has made himself of no reputation.

— Tami Herron

He communicates, "I care about you and I want to be with you."

— Marty Herron

Les doesn't have a proud bone in his body.
He is the most humble man I will ever know.

— Bob Rhodes

Les brought me to a philosophical pivot in my
personal look at the Christian life.

— Marty Von

Thank you, Dr. Ollila, for showing me
real-life Christianity. I love you.

— Rebekah Drake

He is a true example of Christ, no prejudice
and no respecter of persons.

— Sarah Muth

Dr. Ollila has such a great way of helping you put all of your focus on God.

— Linda Lewis

I have learned from Dr. Ollila that "any move on the flow chart" in a ministry is a horizontal one and not a vertical one.

— Ellen Carlson

Dr. Ollila has caused me to recognize and to learn who my God really is.

— Lisa Greiner

Dr. and Mrs. Ollila have made an impact that has stayed as we are honored to serve our Lord here in Argentina.

— Charlie and JoAnn Smith

I cannot believe how well he remembers those of us who have been gone for some time from the campus.

— Theo-Ann Padilla

Doc O lives his life lessons.

— Josh Beers

Les Ollila's genuineness, humility, and a-political approach to serving God, not men, has been a blessing in my life that words cannot express. I truly think of him as a second father.

— Jim Phillips

He always took time to share a cup of coffee; he never seemed rushed even when I know he had more important things waiting.

— Les Heinze

Whenever he shared stories from his past experience, I was assured that this was a man who lived out the Christian life.

— Andy Rupert

He's president of a college, but how many presidents get out and drive pay loaders and help you with menial tasks?

— Doug Bennett

He is real–he relates to people. That would probably be the key.

— Jerry Fair

His professional moves have always been done according to the Lord's will, not according to self-aggrandizement or personal gain. That speaks volumes to me.

— Jim Bennett

His Upper Peninsula demeanor endeared him to many.

— Bill and Sandy Arndt

He is respected by people in the community who found him willing to put on old clothes, grab a chain saw, and help them with something that needed to be done.

— Dennis Walton

So many people in his position sit shuffling papers and they aren't listening to you; he really gives full attention—he looks right at you and he really gets involved.

— Harold and Joan Patz

I find myself quoting him in conversation and messages, but better than that, I sense personal spiritual growth as a result of his life and ministry.

— Ernest Schmidt

My parents came from such knock-you-down backgrounds. That is what has made them such merciful, passionate people.

— Tami (Ollila) Bennett

My dad was a very good father; he doesn't waver on what he believes. It has always been important to him that our needs were met.

— Lisa (Ollila) Swanson

Dr. Ollila preached a message entitled "Hiding Behind a Mask." That first night of Revival Week at NBBC I made a decision to accept Christ. Thank you, Dr. Ollila, for sharing the lesson of the mask.

— Christy Glover

Les was like our son.

— Pastor Charles and Mrs. Hart

I would come home from school, which was two blocks away, and I would see Les and Earl's car and I said, "Oh, good, we are in for some fun!" That was the feeling. I don't ever remember having one feeling of regret my entire life over their visits.

— Carol (Hart) Kersey

*I have been thinking about the saying, "Less is More." In a sense, "***Les** *is more." He is more than the kid from Gratiot, more than any of us would have guessed at that time. A number from our youth group went on to be the people God laid hold of and used in surprising ways.*

— Lois Hart

I remember Pastor Les, as we called him, always being on our side. It wasn't that he always let us have our way, but he always wanted us to know we were loved and he gave us latitude.

— Sandy (Rhodes) Casey

Pastor Les was an encouragement always, and he was just plain fun, too. A great example!

— Sharon (Rhodes) Hall

Charlene and Les always had that open door policy. They knew that the Holy Spirit was prompting them if someone just needed to sit and talk. You don't find that in many pastors.

— Cheryl Hairgrove

I noticed what was so different about Les Ollila when he would speak at conferences with the "big name boys." They would blow in, blow up, and blow out. But Les Ollila would mix and mingle and answer hard questions over a cup of coffee with the guys. I'll never forget that example.

— Jerry Hairgrove

He loved his young people unconditionally. He really is a servant. Place and position mean nothing to him. No politics. What you see is what you get.

— Pam Cushman

Dr. Les Ollila has caused our whole family to grow. The emphasis on being honest and being real and keeping short accounts with God has been a powerful impact on all of us.

— Neal Cushman

God has given Les a gift of discernment and wisdom; he could take scriptures and just make them come alive for all of us.

— Barb Corey

Les never cared if others copyrighted things that he originated. As long as people could use the information, that was fine with him.

— Tim Corey

His casual approach and discernment were incredible. He would take people that were not strong leaders and build them. He taught people by his example.

— Dave Weirich

When Les heard that he was wanted as the president of Northland, he said, "This is like putting whipped cream on an onion." He is truly a humble man.

— Joyce Weirich

I call Dr. O the Vance Havner of our era because God has allowed him to say concisely and concretely a Biblical principle that sticks with you.

— Tom Farrell

Les Ollila has made such an impression on me because he seems so knowing—so sensitive—so in tune with what God is doing and wanting to do in lives.

— Terri Templin

Dr. Ollila is one of the most selfless people that I have ever met.

— Becky Thompson

Les is very open—a man of integrity, honesty, and in every way, very down to earth, very practical, very helpful—he'll bend over backwards again and again and again to help someone. There is no respecter of persons with him.

— Art Raske

His loyalty and servant's heart are "sterling" qualities.

— Rod Bell

No job is too little for him, too menial for him. I remember I was walking around and I looked up and there was the president of the college tree-topping. He is such a humble servant.

— Joy Wagner

He's very relational. He loves telling stories. He'll interact with you if you just stop him on the sidewalk or road.

— Jeff Kahl

Les Ollila has made this ministry what it is:
Friendly, Servant-like, Humble Folks, Down-to-Earth
Mentality, and No Noses up in the Air.

— Jack Noonan

I could not begin to tell you how Dr. Ollila has shaped my life. The Holy Spirit used him to strike a knife into my heart convicting me deeply that my Christian life was very sick. One day, I surrendered fully to the Lord. My life has been one of many trials but truly great joy as well.

— Carol Trahan

The thing that the Lord used for us to come to Northland was what we saw in the dedication and spirit of the students who had a servant's heart; and of course, such a philosophy comes from the leadership which is exemplified in Dr. Les Ollila.

— Ardell and Dottie Jacquot

Les's ministry is far reaching and will extend far beyond his life on earth through the lives of those teens who are now mature adults functioning as pastors, administrators in Christian Schools and lay leaders in churches across America. Carolyn and I have been blessed to know him as both a personal friend and a spiritual leader.

— Dick Leiter

I'd say Les Ollila is transparent, down-to-earth, real, no facade, what you see is what you get, which is a great quality. I think that is the biblical definition of the word sincere.

— Doug McLachlan

BIBLIOGRAPHY

Arndt, Bill. Email interview. 23 May 2002.

Arndt, Sandy. Email interview. 23 May 2002.

Beers, Josh. Email interview. 25 June 2002.

Bell, Rod. Email interview. 6 June 2002.

- - -. *The Mantle of the Mountain Man.* Ed. Becky J. Smith. Greenville, SC: Bob Jones UP, 1999.

Bennett, Doug. Personal interview. May 2002.

Bennett, Jim. Personal interview. 18 June 2002.

Bennett, Tami. Personal interview. 22 July 2002.

Blackstock, Jill. Email interview. 20 May 2002.

Butler, Twila. Personal interview. 21 Aug. 2002.

Carlson, Ellen. Email interview. 6 Aug. 2002.

Casey, Sandy. Email interview. 27 June 2002.

Collard, Timothy. Letter to the author. Apr. 2002.

Corey, Barb. Personal interview. 9 July 2002.

Corey, Timothy. Personal interview. 9 July 2002.

Cushman, Neal. Personal interview. 20 June 2002.

Cushman, Pam. Personal interview. 20 June 2002.

Drake, Rebekah. Email interview. 18 June 2002.

Davis, Fred. Telephone interview. 8 Oct. 2002.

Fair, Jerry. Personal interview. May 2002.

Farrell, Tom. Personal interview. 23 July 2002.

Farrell, Regina. Personal interview. 23 July 2002.

"Ghost Towns of the Keweenaw Peninsula." Online posting. 1999-2001. Ghost Towns of the Upper Peninsula. . . . from the Copper Mining of the 1800s. 24 May 2002 http://www.exploringthenorth.com/ghost/towns.html.

Glover, Christy. Email interview. 22 June 2002.

Greiner, Lisa. Email interview. 9 Aug. 2002.

Hairgrove, Cheryl. Personal interview. 3 July 2002.

Hairgrove, Jerry. Personal interview. 3 July, 2002.

Hall, Sharon. Email interview. 25 June 2002.

Harder, Anna. Email interview. 2 July 2002.

Hart, Charles. Personal interview. 13 May 2002.

Hart, Joyce. Personal interview. 13 May 2002.

Hart, Lois. Letter to the author. 8 June 2002.

- - -. Reading from letters. Audiocassette. 1 July 2002.

Heinze, Les. Email interview. 21 June 2002.

Herron, Marty. Personal interview. 13 July 2002.

Herron, Tami. Personal interview. 13 July 2002.

Hillila, Bernhard. *The Suana Is. . . .* Iowa City, Iowa: Penfield P, 1988.

"History of Bootleg Corner." Mount Calvary Baptist Church. Homepage. 2001. 5 June 2002 http://www.mountcalvarybaptist.org/bootleg.html.

Horn, Sam. Email interview. Nov. 2003.

Jacquot, Ardell. Email interview. 30 Aug. 2002.

Kahl, Jeff. Personal interview. 21 June 2002.

Kersey, Carol. Personal interview. 9 June 2002.

Kimbrough, Wynne. Personal interview. 2 July 2002.

Leiter, Dick. Email interview. 15 Aug. 2002.

Lewis, Linda. Email interview. 13 Aug. 2002.

McLachlan, Doug. Personal interview. 8 Aug. 2002.

Molloy, Lawrence. "Copper Country Road Trips: Enjoy Keweenaw History From The Comfort of Your Car." Online posting. 2001. 24 May 2002 http://www.exploringthenorth.com/coppertrips/guide.html.

"Church Philosophy." Mount Calvary Baptist Church. Homepage. 2002. 5 June 2002. http://www.mountcalvarybaptist.org/philo.html

Monette, Clarence. *Some Copper Country Names and Places.* Lake Linden, MI: Welden H. Curtin, 1975.

Muth, Sarah. Email interview. 2 July 2002.

Noonan, Jack. Email interview. 19 Aug. 2002.

Ollila, Charlene. Personal interview. 6 Oct. 2002.

Ollila, Earl. Personal interview. 10 June 2002.

Ollila, Les. *Calvary Baptist Youth.* Unpublished Youth Notebook.

- - -. *Foundations for Youth Ministry.* Audiocassette. Brevard, NC: The Wilds Christian Camp/Conference Center.

- - -. *Foundations for Youth Programs.* Rocky Mount, NC: Positive Action for Christ, 1981.

- - -. Personal interview. 1 Feb. 2002.

- - -. Quotations. Junior/Senior Banquet. 28 Apr. 2000.

Ollila, Linda. Personal interview. 10 June 2002.

Ollila, Ron. Personal interview. 10 June 2002.

Ollila, Steven. Personal interview. 10 Aug. 2002.

Padilla, Theo-Ann. Email interview. 28 June 2002.

Patz, Harold. Personal interview. 28 June 2002.

Phillips, Jim. Email interview. 25 June 2002.

Porkka, Elaine. Personal interview. 14 May 2002.

Raske, Arthur. Personal interview. 3 June 2002.

Rhodes, Robert. Personal interview. 10 June 2002.

Rhodes, Marsella. Personal interview. 10 June 2002.

Rupert, Andy. Email interview. 18 June 2002.

Schmidt, Ernie. "After the First Year." Unpublished essay, 1984.

- - -. Audiocassette interview. 5 Aug. 2002.

- - -. Letter to the author. 5 Aug. 2002.

"A Short History of Copper Mining." Online posting. 1997–2001. Copper Mining History and Copper Harbor Michigan. 24 May 2002 http://www.exploringthenorth.com/cohistory/cophist.html.

Smith, Charlie. Email interview. 4 July 2002.

Spreitzer, Jack. Personal interview. 13 May 2002.

Star, Jack. "Sweating it out in Finland." *Look* 2002.

Swanson, Lisa. Personal interview. 23 July 2002.

Templin, Terri. Personal interview. 29 May 2002.

Thompson, Becky. Personal interview. 31 May 2002.

Thurner, Arthur. *Calumet Copper and People: History of a Michigan Mining Community, 1864–1970.* Hancock, MI: Book Concern Printers, 1999.

Trahan, Carol. Email interview. 19 Aug. 2002.

"Unlikely Success: The Story of Paul Patz." Dunbar, WI: Northland Baptist Bible College, 2002.

Von, Marty. Personal interview. 21 May 2002.

- - -. Personal interview. 31 May 2002.

Wagner, Joy. Personal interview. 7 June 2002.

Walton, Dennis. Email interview. 14 Aug. 2002.

Weirich, Dave. Personal interview. 9 July 2002.

Weirich, Joyce. Personal interview. 9 July 2002.

Wuori, Beatrice. Telephone interview. Aug. 2002.